THE DOG'S TALE

THE DOG'S TALE

A HISTORY OF MAN'S BEST FRIEND

LOYD GROSSMAN

BBC BOOKS

This book is published to accompany the
television series entitled *The Dog's Tale*
which was first broadcast in autumn 1993

A Union Pictures production for BBC
in association with Arts & Entertainment Network

EXECUTIVE PRODUCERS:
Franc Roddam
Geoff Deehan
Bradley Adams

DIRECTED BY:
Andrew Jackson
Michael Waldman

SERIES PRODUCER:
Michael Waldman

Published by BBC Books,
a division of BBC Enterprises Limited,
Woodlands, 80 Wood Lane
London W12 0TT

First Published 1993
© Union Pictures and Loyd Grossman 1993
The moral rights of the author have been asserted.

ISBN 0 563 36353 3

Designed by Harry Green and Bingley
Set in Baskerville by Selwood Systems, Midsomer Norton
Printed and bound in Great Britain by Butler & Tanner Ltd, Frome and London
Colour separation by Technik Ltd, Berkhamsted
Jacket printed by Lawrence Allen Ltd, Weston-super-Mare

Frontispiece: Spitz
Page 7: Spaniel puppies

CONTENTS

INTRODUCTION

This book was inspired by the desire to find the truth behind a cliché. We all know – and some of us believe it to be true – that 'a dog is man's best friend'. But even a cursory look at the way in which dogs are treated around the world today shows that friendship to be an unusual one. Billions of pounds, dollars and yen are spent on dogs. There are resort hotels where dogs will be hand-fed fillet steak, and boutiques where they can be bought diamond-studded collars. Seemingly intelligent and sophisticated people dress their dogs in pyjamas, kiss them and speak to them in what can only be described as baby talk. Other people, like the Inuit, fishermen of the Arctic and the tribal hunters of Papua New Guinea would find it difficult to survive without the hard work of their huskies and hunting-dogs. Blind people, deaf people and people who cannot get around very well rely on the help of companion dogs. For all of them, and many others, 'Life without a dog is nothing,' as the Irish novelist Elizabeth Bowen observed.

Yet even in the most 'dog loving' societies tens of thousands of dogs are destroyed because there is nothing else to do with them, and in those same societies dogs can be treated with unspeakable cruelty. Elsewhere they are vilified or feared or served for supper. Some friendship.

It is, nevertheless, the most enduring friendship in human history. It has gone on for perhaps 20 000 years. Clearly, as far as we humans are concerned, dogs are unlike any other animal. One of the reasons might be that we invented them by taming wolves and moulding them to fit our needs and fancies. Dogs are fundamentally wild animals that have decided to join the human pack, and as a result we have given them a status that can only be described as that of 'honorary humans.'

We know remarkably little about our best friends. We certainly do not know – and never will – what they think about us, although we like to believe that they love and esteem humans. We certainly know more about our thoughts about them – thoughts which fill this book. Our relationship with the dog has exercised generations of writers, poets, painters and philosophers: no animal has ever gripped the human heart and mind so fiercely. Can anyone watch the perfect interaction between a shepherd and his sheep-dog without feeling that our best friend was also our greatest invention?

This book is not a narrative history of dogs and humans and it makes no attempt to be either complete or definitive. What it does, is explore in a highly subjective way some of the aspects of a very old and very complicated story. It complements and amplifies a television series of the same name which is the most ambitious group of films ever made about how dogs and people have affected each other. My co-writer on the series, Michael Waldman (who was also the series producer), has been a source of great stimulation. Bradley Adams, who was the executive producer of the films, has been – especially in the tentative early months of the series and the book – invaluable for his support and for criticism of the most helpful and rigorous variety. Pratap Rughani (our assistant producer) and Margaret zu Hohenlohe were tireless researchers. Theresa Slowick and the staff of the Kennel Club Library were a great help, as were the staffs of the London Library and the British Library. Sheila Ableman and Tessa Clark of BBC Books have shepherded the author with care and toleration. This book is dedicated with great love to my three girls and two dogs.

Finally, I remind you of S.J. Perelman's wise counsel: 'Outside of a dog, a book is a man's best friend. Inside of a dog it's too dark to read.'

CHAPTER ONE

HONORARY HUMANS

Humans and dogs have lived in intimacy for more than 10 000 years and we still do not know why dogs wag their tails. We are pleased and just a little bit flattered when a dog greets us this way. We assume that it is showing us love and devotion. But is it?

The anthropologist and behaviouralist Desmond Morris offers an unsentimental explanation of what happens when a friendly dog greets its master. Tail wagging, Morris explains, is a sign of emotional conflict. The dog's 'overpowering mood on these occasions is one of friendliness and excitement ... but this attraction is tinged with slight apprehension.' After all, he goes on, we are much bigger than dogs and our size may threaten them. We also decide what and when they eat. To the behaviouralist, a tail-wagging dog is an affectionate dog – and a frightened one. 'We find this hard to accept,' Morris writes, 'because we do not like to think that our dogs have anything but love for us.'

An altogether rosier view of tail wagging comes, surprisingly, from Arthur Schopenhauer, the grim nineteenth-century German philosopher best known for his egoism ('To be alone is the fate of all great minds') and anti-feminism ('The fundamental fault of the female character is that it has no sense of justice'). For him, tail wagging was an expression of pleasure close to human laughter. 'How favourably this form of

Eyes bright, tail wagging,
a dog leaps with 'joy' at its owner's approach. We think
dogs love and understand us, but we still don't
know what they think and why they behave as they do.

greeting ... compares with the obsequious bows and polite grunts of humans,' he observed. 'Dogs are rightly regarded as the epitome of loyalty ... where else shall one find refuge from the endless dissimulation, falsehood and treachery of humans, if not in dogs, upon whose honest countenance one can gaze without mistrust.'

So, do dogs wag their tails as the physical expression of psychological conflict or because they are pleased to see us?

Neither the behaviouralist nor the sentimentalist knows. What we do know is that most dog owners from empresses to shepherds have shared Schopenhauer's view of their animals as a 'refuge'. In the 1989 film *Wall Street* when the villainous Gordon Gekko snarled 'if you want a friend, get a dog' he was merely cynically echoing the sentiments of millions, felt over thousands of years. Sentiments which have endured in spite of the cruel biological fact that a dog's life span is almost certain to be a fraction of his owner's three-score and ten.

DOGS AND HUMAN EMOTIONS

When the nineteenth-century American journalist Ambrose Bierce defined a dog as 'a kind of additional or subsidiary deity designed to catch the overflow and surplus of the world's worship' he was hinting at the fact that it frequently has to carry an almost superabundance of human feelings. Very emotionally reserved societies like England and Japan are often the greatest dog lovers. Dogs may provide an outlet for emotions that we dare not show to our fellow humans. They are also emotionally 'easy'. We can depend on them because their feelings towards us are meant to be immutable, incorruptible and more certain than death or taxes.

Only in the last ten years has anyone bothered to ask whether that sort of relationship is fair to the dog. A breeder made what seemed like a shocking statement to *The Times* when she said: 'Dogs are made the repository of too many human anxieties, too much tension and too much stress from trying to be what a dog was never intended to be: a sponge to soak up human emotions.'

This emotional dependency can work both ways. Anyone who has ever grieved over the death of a pet dog will know that the feelings aroused are often as strong and persistent as those that are caused by human death. The growth of counselling and support groups for mourning dog owners has now spread well beyond their spiritual home in California. Rudyard Kipling, who never pulled a sentimental punch, wrote a masterful précis of the lover's tragedy that man and dog enact.

> Buy a pup and your money will buy,
> Love unflinching that cannot lie –
> Perfect passion and worship fed,
>   By a kick in the ribs or a pat on the head.
> Nevertheless it is hardly fair,
>   To risk your heart for a dog to tear.

It is this 'perfect passion and worship' that has always fuelled the man and dog relationship. When Aldous Huxley observed that to every dog his master is a Napoleon, he grasped only half of the relationship. To every master, his dog is more than an animal. To every master, his dog, and his dog alone, is nearly human.

Nowhere is the dog's unique status as a sort of honorary human more obvious than in death when dogs have been monumentalized and eulogized with a fervour we sometimes fail to accord to our fellow humans. In November 1808 the aristocratic household of Newstead Abbey, Nottinghamshire, was plunged into mourning when Boatswain, a five-year-old Newfoundland, had a fit and died. His inconsolable master sat down to write an epitaph for his late pet describing the dog as:

> … in life the firmest friend,
>   The first to welcome, foremost to defend.
> Whose honest heart is still his master's own,
>   Who labours, fights, lives and breathes for him alone.

Certainly not Lord Byron's finest poetry, but among his most heartfelt. The twenty-year-old Byron had already established himself as a flamboyant character at Cambridge University. When the fellows of Trinity College tried to prevent Boatswain from living in Byron's rooms, the poet retaliated by presenting a trained bear as a candidate for a college fellowship. The bear was rejected, but the dog was allowed to stay.

Boatswain's premature death unleashed a flood of histrionics: 'Boatswain is dead!' Byron wrote to a friend. 'I have now lost everything except Murray.' Murray, by the way, was his favourite household servant, not his publisher John Murray. Byron spent the then considerable sum of £260 erecting an elaborate monument to his dog – and rewrote his will specifying that he should be buried alongside Boatswain, and the faithful Murray, in a vault beneath it.

Although dog monuments were mildly eccentric in Byron's time, they were hardly unknown. In her journal of 1781 Lady Dimsdale, an Englishwoman at the Russian court, writes: 'I was surprised to see in a retired part of the garden a fine pyramid which I was informed could not have been built for less than two thousand pounds.' The pyramid was the tomb of three of Catherine the Great's greyhounds. Back in England, the mid-eighteenth-century Temple of British Worthies built at Stowe House for Viscount Cobham celebrates the life of 'Signor Fido', an Italian greyhound, alongside the achievements of Shakespeare, Newton and Bacon. Fido, we are told, was 'a perfect Philosopher, a faithful Friend, an agreeable Companion'. So Boatswain's mausoleum was part of an established aristocratic practice of funerary architecture for beloved pet dogs. Byron and others who were highly privileged could express, and consequently relieve, their anguish through such grand gestures. More modest dog owners had to content themselves with private mourning. The recent development of commercial pet cemeteries mimics the grandeur of Boatswain's mausoleum, Signor Fido's temple and the imperial greyhounds' pyramid.

Byron and his beloved Newfoundland 'Boatswain' – the poet's 'firmest' friend – were clumsily frozen in bloodless adoration by the sculptor Richard Belt for an 1880 memorial in London (*left*). Friends considered it a poor likeness of both man and dog.

By the time Richard Ansdell (1815–55) painted this heroic Newfoundland (*right*) the breed was beginning to become popular with middle-class British dog owners: the family of the novelist Anthony Trollope owned one.

Byron's friend John Cam Hobhouse wrote an introduction to Boatswain's epitaph which became a classic of canine literature. It eulogizes the dog as one 'Who possessed Beauty without vanity, Strength without indolence, Courage without ferocity. And all the virtues of Man, without his Vices.' Alas, Byron had to sell Newstead Abbey in 1813 so neither he nor the long-serving Murray ever joined Boatswain in the vault. However, master and dog are almost equally prominent in a monumental bronze statue of the poet in London's Hyde Park.

Hobhouse was echoing a sentiment that had been fashionable in progressive intellectual circles for much of the previous century. As the idea of the noble savage uncorrupted by civilization – first promoted by the French philosopher Rousseau as the foundation for his political theories – gained popularity, the dog had come to be seen as another sort of noble savage. All the more lovable, perhaps, for not being human. In spite of the dog's intimacy with man it remained an exemplar of primeval goodness. Unsurprisingly, the *philosophes* of the Age of Reason were particularly full of praise for dogs: Voltaire said, 'The best thing about man is the dog'. The Romantic poet Lamartine remarked that the more he saw of people the more he admired dogs. These sentiments were echoed and amplified. Although dog owners may be accused of treating their pets as surrogate humans, it might be more accurate to say that dogs have often been held up by writers, philosophers and artists as idealized humans. 'Histories are more full of examples of the fidelity of dogs than of friends,' the poet Alexander Pope wrote.

DOGS AND THE POWERFUL

Dogs have been associated with the powerful since the invention of political states in the ancient Middle East. A series of bas-reliefs commissioned for the palace of Nineveh in *c.*645 BC are devoted to a synoptic depiction of the highly ritualized lion, gazelle and wild ass hunts orchestrated by the Assyrian King Ashurbanipal. All three animals disrupted the everyday life of rural Assyria: lions killed livestock and farmers alike,

These seventh-century stone bas-reliefs of mastiff-like animals from the palace of the Assyrian ruler Ashurbanipul in Nineveh are some of the most powerful portraits of ancient dogs. Propagandists made extensive use of the king's skill at hunting and his animals' perfect devotion.

The LINE of BEAUTY

gazelles and wild asses ate crops and trampled fields. The king's performance as first huntsman symbolized both his bravery and his care for his subjects' welfare. Not only did he hunt, he had to be seen to do so. Whether recorded in bas-relief or staged in huge arenas, Ashurbanipal's hunts were object lessons for the Assyrian populace in the king's power and magnificence. These events required large numbers of dogs which appear to be mastiffs. The vividness of the carving testifies to the savagery of these heavily muscled beasts as they corner and attack their prey. Importantly, the behaviour of the royal dogs showed what the king expected from his subjects: obedience and loyalty.

For royal families, especially in times of turmoil and intrigue, dogs have always been valuable for this symbolic role as ideal subjects as well as for their guarding ability and companionship. Their devoted behaviour towards their masters has been a pointed reminder to courtiers and *hoi polloi* alike; they have almost invariably been cosseted members of any royal entourage – and frequently adopted as the badges of court factions and political parties.

The flat-faced, stertorous pug first came to prominence during The Netherlands' struggle for independence from the Spanish empire, when the insistent barking of Prince William the Silent's pet foiled a Spanish assassination attempt in 1572. The pug – small and fierce – immediately came to symbolize the tough little House of Orange, fearlessly nipping at the heels of the Spanish leviathan. When William's great-grandson ascended the English throne in 1689 as William III, the silky coated spaniels favoured by the Stuarts were quickly replaced by the Dutch pugs and the fashion for owning them was established, spreading beyond court circles.

The painter Hogarth was one of the most enthusiastic pug owners of his time and frequently used his dogs, Trump and Pug, as models in paintings and engravings, whose huge sales further popularized the breed. The eighteenth century is, in fact, full of famous owners of pugs, from Louis XV's mistress Madame du Barry – whose favourite, Dorine, wore a gold collar with a diamond-studded locket – to Josephine

The most incisive observer of the high and low life of Georgian England, William Hogarth (1697–1764) frequently included dogs in his moral paintings and portraits of English families. His own passion was for pugs. Trump, his favourite, shares pride of place in this 1745 self-portrait.

de Beauharnais' Fortune who was alleged to have bitten Napoleon in a bedroom scuffle. In 1740 the elector of Cologne even established a chivalric order whose badge was a gold pug.

A pug, Bully, was the only dog allowed to sleep on Queen Victoria's bed. Although she actually favoured Pomeranians, her royal household was home to a number of

The barely detectable
smile makes this one of the warmest photographs
of the remote, widowed Queen Victoria. It was taken
at Balmoral, her Scottish retreat, in 1867.

breeds. Her love of dogs and her patronage of the painter Sir Edwin Landseer contributed vastly to the rather sentimental adoration of dogs that still marks Anglo-American cultures and those influenced by them. As the sovereign who added 'Royal' to the Society for the Prevention of Cruelty to Animals, her feelings for 'our poor, dear friends, the dogs' were well known. She wrote forcefully to Disraeli demanding stricter regulation of the then rapidly growing use of dogs in medical experiments. The queen's feelings were part of the change in public feeling about cruelty to animals which led to the enactment of the Cruelty to Animals Act of 1876. Although the Act introduced a licensing system for experiments using live animals it sadly failed to seriously reduce the number that were painful.

Victoria's most sensational pet was Lootie, a Pekingese presented to her by an army officer, Captain John Dunne, after the looting of the Chinese Summer Palace by French and British troops towards the end of the Second Opium War in 1860. The attack on the palace was a shocking end to a shameful war fought to force China to allow her citizens to be ravaged by imported opium and her sovereignty to be eroded: the palace's serene magnificence was reduced to shattered porcelain, torn silk and murdered courtiers. Many of the court dogs were slain by their keepers to prevent their capture by the Westerners, but five survived the carnage and were treated with solicitude by the victors. Captain Dunne brought one of them back to England and wrote to his queen offering the 'most affectionate and intelligent little creature' as a souvenir of Her Majesty's far-reaching power.

Lootie's international odyssey was not unusual. Rare and interesting breeds of dogs were frequently spoils of war or gifts from one potentate to another. James I of England sent six 'little white earth dogges' or Scottish terriers to his father-in-law the king of Denmark and Pekingese themselves may have first arrived in China as presents from the Byzantine court at Constantinople.

As Buddhism became the religion of the Chinese court the Pekingese's very slight resemblance to a lion – an animal unknown in China, but key to Buddhist mythology – made it particularly prized. By the seventeenth century, the time of the Manchu emperors, the imperial Pekingese were an essential part of court life. They were bred with a fanatical attention to colour: a black dog with white ears was a sign of wealth and nobility, a yellow dog with white forelegs was good luck, and so on. Attended by eunuchs and moved between palaces in jade and enamel cages of fantastic elaboration,

DOGS OF THE ORIENT

The first recognizable Pekingese may have been bred in China 2000 years ago but, as with many breeds of great antiquity, their origins are murky. As palace dogs they enjoyed incredibly high status, transported in jewelled cages, eating a refined diet and sometimes slumbering in the sleeves of high officials.

Although Pekingese were the breed most highly valued by the Chinese imperial household, other kinds of dog were carefully bred and maintained. This Tang Dynasty (AD 618–907) hound would have been kept for hunting.

BELOW *Pugs are widely believed to be relatives of the Pekingese, with longer legs and smooth coats. These puppies were immortalized in porcelain by a Japanese craftsman.*

ABOVE *The colour of a Pekingese was full of symbolic significance to the imperial Chinese. Today, connoisseurship of 'Pekes' still involves a highly developed appreciation of the colours of their fine, silky coats.*

Guardians of the gates
of paradise, these Foo or lion
dogs were thought to be the
mythic ancestors of the
Pekingese.

RIGHT *After European troops sacked
the Summer Palace near Peking in 1860
the imperial dogs were displayed to a
European audience for the first time.
Looty was presented to Queen Victoria
as part of the spoils of war.*

the life of the Pekingese reflected the remote artificiality of Chinese palace culture. Victoria's contemporary, the Dowager Empress Tzu Hsi, described the diet of one of her dogs: 'Shark's fins, curlews' livers and the breasts of quails on these it may be fed; and for drink, give it the tea that is brewed from the spring buds of the shrub that groweth in the province of Hankow, or the milk of the antelope, that pasture in the Imperial park.' Begrudged even her modest, but preferred, diet of a little minced chicken and breadcrumbs, Lootie was subject to a rather harsher life when she joined the borzois, collies, dachshunds and beagles of Victoria's household.

DOGS AND THE FAMILY

By the time of Lootie's arrival at Buckingham Palace the allegorical role of the royal dog had changed. The depoliticizing of royal courts meant that dogs were no longer used as symbols of courtly fidelity or as idealized subjects. At a time when Victoria and Albert began to present the image of themselves and their children as an exemplary family, dogs began to be regarded as indispensable members of any respectable household.

The ownership of dogs as pets spread throughout the industrialized countries. As more families made more money in new commercial and industrial pursuits that were increasingly distanced from raw nature, the demand for pets grew. Inventive capitalism responded. James Spratt, an Ohio-born commercial traveller in lightning conductors, began to manufacture 'Spratt's Meal Fibrine Dog Cakes' in 1860. The marketing of such commercially prepared dog food, along with books and periodicals like *The Ladies' Kennel Journal* which popularized knowledge about dogs and their care, both reflected and contributed to the growing middle-class trend for keeping dogs as pets.

The pet dog population of countries like Britain, France, Germany and the United States rose steadily, as did the demand for more exotic and highly bred animals. A *Punch* cartoon of 1889 lampooned the trend with illustrations of the 'Dorgupin,' 'Crocadachshund' and 'Hippotamian Bulldog'. At a time when a large and widely

Pekingese developed
into a recognizable form hundreds of years ago.
The Pekes in this late eighteenth-century painting would
not be out of place at a modern dog show.

DOG FASHIONS FOR 1889.

DORGUPINE, CROCODACHSHUND, POMME-DE-TERRIER (BLACK-AND-TAN), VENTRE-À-TERRIER (SCOTCH), HIPPOPOTAMIAN BULLDOG, GERMAN SAUSAGE DOG, HEDGE-DOG, BUG-DOG.   (*By Our Special Dog-fancier.*)

Dog breeding and showing
was a serious business in Victorian England. Human ideas about fashion
and a high level of consciousness about pets and class led to the creation
of more and more outlandish breeds as *Punch* observed in 1889 (*above*).

Queen Victoria's devotion to her dogs was
lifelong and constant. Sir Edward Landseer gained fame, fortune and a knighthood
thanks to the potent combination of his talent and her patronage. A copy of
a family portrait by Landseer (*left*) shows three of her dogs: Dash, Hector and Nero.

spread middle class was first indulging in 'conspicuous consumption' dogs were becoming a symbol of economic and social status to more people than ever before.

Money was lavished on food, clothing and shelter as dogs increasingly reflected the wealth, influence and stylishness of their masters. Pets of the powerful have always had luxurious fittings and accoutrements − Madame du Barry was hardly the first person to lavish jewels on a dog. The Athenian general Alcibiades famously collared his with solid gold, as did Louis XI of France whose favourite greyhound, Cherami, wore a gold and ruby collar. Inevitably, the currency of luxury became debased. As regal dogs were treated more like members of the family, middle-class dogs were showered with luxuries and the pampering of dogs was transformed from a courtly fancy into a bourgeois industry.

Today, in the chic 16th arrondissement of Paris, the Kennel Club boutique bakes chocolate and beef gâteaus for dogs and sells sartorial horrors like gold lamé evening gowns in a variety of dog sizes. American shops sell pooch ponchos ('Features . . . windproof tail strap'), hooded snow-suits ('Zinger pink or neon yellow trimmed with black') and sunglasses ('Practical and FUN for all cool dogs'). These products echo the jade dog-cages of the Manchus, but seem faintly ridiculous as mass-market mail-order goods aimed at suburban families.

Over-indulgent owners may even take their dogs on special holidays. At the Idol Pet Heaven in Fukuoka, Japan, the 'Most luxurious and wonderful holidays are provided with every luxury imaginable for your pets!' as the brochure exclaims. 'Luxury in our cultural life has spread into the everyday life of our pets.' The New

A rich velvet cushion, a
handsomely crafted collar and a noble profile all signal the
elevated status of this small greyhound, a pet of Frederick
the Great. Supposedly developed in ancient Egypt,
this breed has frequently been a monarchical favourite.

York owner of some bichon frises told the *Sunday Telegraph* that she was planning to fly her dogs to Paris: 'It's very chic to bring your dog to a restaurant in Europe.'

DOGS AS FOOD

It is less chic, perhaps even insensitive, to bring your dog to a restaurant in East Asia where one of his relatives might be on the menu. Eating dog is one of the world's great cultural divides. European and North Americans regard eating the flesh of dogs as akin to cannibalism and this has often been cited as evidence of the way we define them as being different from all other animals – in fact, closer to humans. However, dog eating is pretty well distributed through space and time. It has been widespread in sub-Saharan Africa and across Polynesia. Pre-Columbian shaft tombs in Colima, western Mexico have yielded a number of beautifully modelled clay dogs buried with their masters. Were the dogs of Colima meant to guide the dead through the underworld or were they buried as a post-mortem snack? Even though dogs were one of the few domesticated animals of ancient Central America, and prized as pets and hunting companions, they frequently ended their lives in the cooking pot.

Contemporary dog eating is most highly developed in China and Korea. As with the pre-Columbian peoples, dog eaters are often owners. 'It doesn't bother me at all,' a Korean dog owner said tucking into a plate of braised dog. 'It's not my dog that I'm eating.' Chinese and Korean governments, worried about Western public opinion, have sometimes tried to intervene. A reformist Chinese regime unsuc-

The inhabitants of Colima in western Mexico produced a number of vivacious and beautifully crafted clay figures to bury in shaft tombs. This dog, probably made between AD 200 and 600, represented a good hunting companion as well as an occasional source of food.

cessfully banned dog eating in 1915, and at the time of the 1988 Seoul Olympics the Korean Government suppressed dog restaurants. They almost all reopened when the bulk of foreign tourists had gone home.

Dog is a delicacy in both countries and the Chinese, especially, feel it has important medicinal value. A Hong Kong resident told an American anthropologist that it was an important part of his winter diet and quoted a saying that, 'If you eat dog you will keep warm all the time'. While the Chinese will cook and eat most breeds, the sturdy, black-tongued chow is the most favoured. The use of 'chow' as the English slang for food is a macabre memento of the breed's most common use. When the first chows arrived in Britain in the eighteenth century, the naturalist and curate Gilbert White noted without a hint of moral censure that a neighbour of his 'brought home a dog and a bitch of the Chinese breed from Canton; such as are fattened in that country for the purpose of being eaten.' In general, young dogs are preferred for culinary purposes and in some restaurants and markets caged puppies are kept ready for the pot. While we find this repulsive, and indeed morally objectionable, it is worth remembering that in a dog-loving society like Britain more than 1000 unwanted dogs are put to death every week.

The Chinese attitude towards dogs embodies many of the paradoxes that all cultures feel about our best friends. On the one hand, they have enthusiastically dined on them for some centuries: on the other, no dogs were more assiduously documented or lavished with luxury than those of the imperial court. Other societies have loved and vilified dogs with equal passion. The mad dog, the devil dog, the hell hound are all as full of cultural and emotional resonances as the more comforting image of the family dog stretched out on the hearthrug. A wolf lurks inside even the most highly coiffed Pekingese. The whole shared history of man and dog involves controlling and manipulating the characteristics of a wild animal in the effort to create a civilized, useful and companionable beast.

Writing in the first century BC Cicero praised dogs: 'Such fidelity of dogs in protecting what is committed to their charge. Such affectionate attachment to their masters. Such jealousy of strangers. Such acuteness of nose in following a track. Such keenness in hunting. What else do they evince, but that these animals were created for the use of man.'

But when – and how?

CHAPTER TWO

MAN MEETS DOG

L a Fontaine, the seventeenth-century French fable writer, used dogs in many of his moral tales. In one of them a wolf crept into a farmyard looking for a chicken or two. He was met by an angry dog and abandoning his larcenous plans sat down for a chat. He admired the dog's sleek coat, warm bed and general air of contentment. 'Tell me brother,' he asked the dog, 'how do you manage do have it so easy?' 'Well,' the dog explained, 'the farmer and I have a bargain. I guard his house and his chickens and his sheep and he feeds me well and gives me a nice place to sleep.' Just as the wolf was about to ask how he could make the same arrangement, he noticed that the dog was wearing something around his neck. 'What on earth's that thing?' 'That's my collar,' the dog replied, and went on to explain how his master could attach a rope to it to tie him up. The wolf looked at him in horror and ran off into the night.

In spite of their differences, wolves and dogs are nearly identical animals. In fact, you could say that dogs are wolves who have made a behavioural bargain with man. When humans and wolves began their tentative steps towards partnership many thousands of years ago the domestic dog was the end result.

Our biological kinship to dogs is distant. We are as closely related to them as we are to cows, for example. Indeed, dogs are more closely related to cats than they are

S ilky coated, dewy eyed, diminutively
built, Yorkshire terriers seem a world away from their ancestor the wolf.
But in spite of years of selective breeding to be ornamental they share
bravery, cunning and a killing instinct with their wild relative.

to humans. Nevertheless, over the millenia we have been close to them functionally and psychologically, even if not biologically.

Dogs and wolves are both members of the subgroup of mammals known as carnivores, a big and aggressive order of intelligent, flesh-eating predators with clawed toes and well-developed teeth for tearing, crushing and cutting. Their earliest identifiable ancestors appeared on Earth about seventy million years ago. The carnivores are divided further into two superfamilies: the *Canidae* and *Felidae*. *Felidae* include the cat, civet and hyena families; the *Canidae* include the dog, bear, sea lion, weasel, seal and racoon families. Biologists divide the *Canidae* into a number of subgenera which include groups of dogs, wolves and foxes. Dogs, wolves, coyotes and jackals are all members of one subgenus – *Canis* (the canids) – a huge and interesting family spread all over the world from desert to ice-flow. One can generalize about their characteristics by saying that they have particularly robust skulls with formidable teeth that are used not just for eating but as weapons. Their legs are built for long-distance running.

In 1758, when the Swedish biologist Carl Linnaeus drew up the system for classifying animals that is still in use, he designated the dog as *Canis familiaris* and the wolf as *Canis lupus*. In fact, it is difficult to make a taxonomic distinction between the wolf and the dog because all the behavioural and physical differences between the two animals are merely the consequences of the wolf's domestication by humans.

I pity the poor wolf turned into an object of hatred and fear by a thousand myths and stories like Little Red Riding Hood or by the familiar Hollywood cliché of wolves circling a camp-fire. Everything we love about our domestic dog – its intelligence, its physical prowess, its love of society – exists somewhere within the wolf.

The great-grandaddy, as it were, of the wolf may have been an ungainly looking creature called *Cynodictus* who first appeared about thirty million years ago. With a long, low-slung body, shortish legs and an extravagant tail he was not much to look at, but he was an intelligent and efficient predator: he survived and his descendants

Charles Dickens adored Little Red Riding Hood and shuddered at the 'cruelty and treachery of that dissembling wolf who ate her grandmother'. Red Riding Hood – illustrated here by Walter Crane – is one of many fairy-tales and legends that cast the shy, relatively harmless wolf as a threatening monster.

Out set Riding Hood, so obliging and
sweet,
And she met a great Wolf in the wood,
Who began most politely the maiden to
greet,
as tender a voice as he could.

He asked to what house she was going,
and why:
Red Riding Hood answered him all:
He said, "Give my love to your Gran; I
will try
"At my earliest leisure to call."

The canids are a highly adaptable, far-flung and varied looking family of hunting animals. The silver-backed jackal (*right*) the coyote (*left*) and the side-striped jackal (*above*) are close but 'uncivilized' relatives of our domestic dogs.

flourished and evolved. Legs became longer, tails became shorter, the five toes on each foot became four. One characteristic remained almost the same, though: the pattern of *Cynodictus'* teeth is almost identical to that of modern dogs and wolves.

Perhaps as early as two million years ago the wolf as we know it had evolved. It was a superbly designed predator with a keen sense of smell and sight, the ability to run as fast as twenty-five miles an hour and, of course, powerful jaws armed with fearsome teeth. As with other canids, there was a short, relatively hard-to-clog-up alimentary canal: small wonder that to eat gluttonously is 'to wolf'.

At about the same time that wolves were evolving, so were the animals that became their main prey: the ungulates – hooved animals like horses, elephants, deer and cattle. Ungulates are generally much bigger than wolves so wolves developed the pack method of hunting in which a team of animals would pursue and kill their prey. Their success as a society of nomadic hunters brought them into early contact and competition with another group of social hunters: humans.

We do not know where or when humans began to take an interest in wolves. The timing of all the great events of pre-history – the invention of fire, for example – is of necessity speculative. The first domestic dogs are generally dated from about 12 000 to 15 000 years ago, but long before that men began to observe wolves and to take an interest in them. Human shelters built within the cave of La Grotte du Lazaret in the south of France some 125 000 years ago are decorated with wolf skulls. The beautiful and sensitive cave paintings found at Lascaux in France or Altamira in Spain show us that Stone Age man had a tremendous empathy with the animals he preyed upon; he and they were, after all, locked into a life and death relationship. The use of wolf skulls at La Grotte du Lazaret may demonstrate that man somehow recognized the wolf as his animal opposite number. Maybe men and wolves somehow began to hunt together. They certainly began to flirt, and wolves must have realized that, like them, men lived in a pack with a well-defined social hierarchy.

So how and when did the wolf come into the human pack?

We need to focus on the upper palaeolithic period just after the peak of the last ice age when the great glaciers were slowly retreating a little under 18 000 years ago. Paradoxically, as Juliet Clutton Brock has pointed out, man is 'a tropical, omniverous primate whose exceptional success as a species began to accelerate only when he became a social hunter in a sub-arctic environment.' In other words, far from his tropical birthplace in Africa, man faced up to the unfamiliar challenges of the ice age and did well.

By the time that the great glacial sheets of ice began their northerly retreat, our prehistoric ancestors had evolved into modern man – *Homo sapiens* – and looked like us. Men and women wore clothes, made tools, talked, sang, buried their dead, cooked, drew pictures and played with their children. They were well-established, confident animals. Men had also become so good at making simple weapons and hunting in groups that many of the large mammals they hunted were on the brink of extinction. But human life remained hard, uncertain and dangerous. In spite of all man's social and technical skills, survival in the small communities of nomadic hunters owed much to luck. Would there always be animals to kill or plants to eat? Would blazing heat or freezing rain drive humans far from their familiar haunts? About five million men, women and children were scattered across the world and life for them must often have been lonely and mysterious. Man needed a friend and a helper. Because their abilities and behaviour were in many ways either similar, or complementary, to those of man, wolves were the ideal candidates.

AN EPOCH-MAKING EPISODE

By the upper palaeolithic period wolves and men had been hunting and living in close proximity for some thousands, even tens of thousands, of years. It is likely that wolves had long scavenged around the margins of human campsites; they were perhaps a little wary of man, but hardly fearful. These big animals – a wolf is about as long as a man is tall – were a familiar part of daily life all over the world. Now comes the great mystery. Some time, say about 15 000 or 20 000 years ago, somewhere, maybe in the Middle East or northern Europe, a wolf cub was 'adopted' by a human family. It was, as Konrad Lorenz wrote, 'an epoch-making episode, a stroke of genius whose meaning in world history is greater than that of the fall of Troy or the discovery of

The wolf (*overleaf*) was the raw material from which man made the dog. The two animals still share a strong sense of social order and the powerful jaws and keen senses that made them successful hunters and hunting companions.

37

gunpowder.' This adoption became in its way a declaration of man's mastery of the world around him. It was the first tentative step towards the creation of what is essentially a man-made animal: the dog.

The ability to domesticate animals changed the history of the world. While it hardly removed all the vicissitudes of life, domestication – of dogs, of sheep, of goats and cattle – created reliable sources of food and raw materials for clothing and made the settled life possible. Consequently, it also made possible the creation of the whole realm of activities and beliefs that we call civilization. So we ought to understand something about how domestication, whether of a wolf cub or a goat, works.

A domestic animal is one which has in a manner of speaking surrendered to man. Its human masters will determine when and with whom it breeds, where it roams – if it roams at all – and what it will eat. Removed from the wild, it becomes increasingly incapable of returning there and soons begin to adapt physically to its new conditions. This is partly why domesticated animals look different from their wild forebears.

The motive behind domestication is usually profit or utility to man. The utility aspect of the relationship is sometimes rather one-sided. Cattle will be treated well until the time comes to slaughter them. Other animals with renewable resources – such as sheep which can be sheared regularly – will have longer lives. In spite of the fact that cruelty to animals has probably been with us since domestication began, it has been widely recognized that well-treated animals are more useful to man than ill-treated ones. Because the dog is one of the few domesticated animals that offers companionship as well as serving some useful role, it has always been more highly prized and pampered than any other.

AND MAN CREATED DOG

Although the fox in La Fontaine's fable valued his spartan freedom above the dog's luxurious enslavement, the dog has entered into a fair bargain with man. But no matter how comfortable an animal's captivity may be, it will still alter its behaviour and its size and shape. When this is coupled with the fact that its masters choose its breeding partners, you can understand that the domestication of any animal is very much the creation of almost a new one to suit the needs of man.

Let us go back to our wolf cub, who was undoubtedly amiable, playful and delightful to look at. Raised by humans, it grew into a wolf who was completely at

Wolves have open, communicative faces.

No one knows where or when humans first tried to domesticate them but we speculate that

the appealing look of a cub must have spoken to a human heart as long as 20 000 years ago.

DOG COLLARS

The dog collar is a mark of subservience and control,
but also of friendship and human devotion.
Much time, ingenuity and money has been expended on
these respectable pieces of dog jewellery.

RIGHT
*A selection of dog collars. In Victorian times
brass ones were sold by street traders – often
with padlocks as optional extras.*

*This French bronze collar,
made c.1800, is decorated with
a fashionable 'Adam'-style
motif of urns and griffins.*

LEFT *This handsome, mid-eighteenth century
Meissen pug sports a purple collar decorated
with apple-shaped, enamelled baubles.*

A brass and iron collar from Germany, c. 1700.

Like feudal servants, dogs wore their
masters' monograms and coats of arms.
This collar was made c. 1700.

LEFT *The collar worn by the lap-dog
in Giovanna Garzoni's seventeenth-
century painting adds a touch of nobility
to a rather preposterous little creature.*

*A selection of collars. From top: Italian brass
collar, c.1630–50; a heavy, leather collar
from Germany, 1779; an iron hunting collar,
also from Germany, seventeenth century; an
Austrian leather collar covered in red velvet
with copper-gilt, mid-eighteenth century.*

RIGHT *The dandified dog was well catered
for in Foin's assortment of collars, on sale
to dog-loving Parisians in 1900.*

DEMI-GRANDEUR

ease in human society. A wolf who was useful in the hunt or as an exemplary look-out. This led to humans adopting – possibly by kidnapping – more wolf cubs. Inevitably, they began to choose ones they liked the look of and, simply by doing that, established the rudiments of breeding.

Breeding allows us to select the characteristics we wish to perpetuate. As soon as man began to domesticate animals he wanted to make them look distinctly different from wild stock. If you had a domesticated wolf, for example, you would want to be able to recognize it instantly. As a result, wolf cubs in captivity were bred with an eye towards giving them coats of a uniform colour. Wolves carry their tails hanging down, so man took great care to breed domesticated ones with instantly recognizable upright or curly tails. Domestication generally makes animals smaller. As a consequence, the wolf as domesticated by man was not as big as its wild counterpart; it was more likely to have a single colour coat; it had an upright or curly tail. It still had the same sort of teeth, although its smaller jaw made them rather crowded.

In spite of The Three Little Pigs and other literary testaments to the wolf's murderous nature, wolves, although superb predators, are not particularly aggressive. A high level of aggression would be unsustainable within the co-operative social system that is the pack. It is a reasonable assumption that domesticated wolves, while meant to be affectionate and loyal to their master and his family, were also bred to be aggressive both for the hunt and to serve as guards.

Notably, the domesticated wolf barked. Wolves in the wild bark only occasionally – when a stranger encroaches on their territory, for example. Most often they communicate through whimpering, growling or howling. Man decided that the ability to bark was useful: it made a splendid alarm if his group's territory was being trespassed. So wolves with a propensity to bark were mated. Another odd 'side-effect' of domestication was a change in their walk. Wolves lope, with their forelegs and hind legs moving along the same line. Dogs walk differently with their hind legs moving in a line outside their forelegs' track.

So we have answers to most of the questions about why man chose the wolf to become his closest animal associate. They all appear to be straightforward and functional. And we have seen some of the consequences of domestication. We know that the physiology and social behaviour of the wolf made it an ideal hunting companion for man during the late ice age and period of glacial retreat. But something more than 'mere' utility created the powerful psychological bond between man and the wolf's descendants that has lasted all these many thousands of years.

Wolves have very open and expressive faces and, like man, tend to use facial communication more than most animals. There is a sense – and I believe that it is more than mere anthropomorphic fancy – that members of the wolf family understand us. Clutton Brock quotes the observations of Sir Francis Galton, the Victorian anthropologist and cousin of Charles Darwin: 'A man irritates a dog by an ordinary laugh, he frightens him by an angry look, or he calms him by a kindly bearing; but he has less spontaneous hold over an ox or a sheep ... He has no natural power at all over many other creatures. Who, for instance, ever succeeded in frowning away a mosquito, or in pacifying an angry wasp by a smile?' Who, indeed. I like Galton's phrase 'natural power' because it neatly hints that the man-dog relationship is based on co-operation and empathy rather than brute mastery and subservience.

In many important ways the new, man-created animal was identical to the wolf. For example, its genetic information was still carried by the same number of chromosomes: seventy-eight. But this new animal was no longer a wolf. It was a dog.

THE ARCHAEOLOGICAL EVIDENCE

The steps leading up to the creation of the dog are all hypothetical. They are based, of course, on our knowledge of the physiology and behaviour of the wolf and on the habits of prehistoric man, but for all that they are just theory. In spite of much theorizing the debate – likely never to be resolved – still rages about where it all happened. There are partisans for China, the Near East, northern Europe or North America who say the domestication of the wolf was a unique event and that the dog spread around the world from one home. Others, including myself, believe the dog is polygenetic in origin and that the process of domestication took place in various locations around the world. The archaeological evidence is widespread although the difficulty of interpreting physical remains to decide what is a wolf and what is a dog bedevils the issue. Certainly, there is very little evidence that what we would recognize as domesticated dogs existed much before 10 000 years ago.

Many of the most interesting early dog remains have been discovered in North America. Enthusiasts are ever hopeful that the rich archaeological site at Old Crow in the Alaskan Yukon, which lies along the route by which Asiatic people first emigrated from Siberia to the Americas about 40 000 years ago, will produce some startling canine find that will push the date of domestication further back into pre-history. However, although bone fragments found there may take it as far back as 30 000 years ago, the most highly studied and widely recognized remains of an early domesticated dog come from a much later site at Jaguar Cave in south-western Idaho. This yielded a number of bones which show that at least two sizes of domesticated dogs lived in the cave when it was inhabited by Amerindians over a 2000-year period beginning more than 10 000 years ago.

The oldest relatively complete dog skeleton, though, comes from a Near Eastern site at Ein Mallaha in Israel which has been dated to around 12 000 years ago. Ein Mallaha was one of many small villages close to or along the Mediterranean shore which are known to archaeologists as Natufian communities. These provide us with many insights into life during the transitional period between the time when men lived as hunter-gatherers and the time when they settled down as agriculturalists. Grindstones found in these villages show that wild wheat was gathered and ground into a coarse foodstuff. There is also evidence of the domestication of animals as well as evidence that the Natufians hunted gazelle and fished. They were able to make and use relatively sophisticated tools.

The human residents of Ein Mallaha lived in a tightly knit community of fifty to sixty round huts; and the archaeological record appears to show that they had strong bonds of affection with their dogs. One of the village tombs yielded a human skeleton buried with that of a four-to-five-month-old puppy. The elderly human's left hand lay gently on its companion's rib-cage. Possibly the puppy had been sacrificed to accompany its master in the afterlife. While archaeologists admit the difficulty of separating dogs from wolves on the basis of bones alone, it would appear from its part in a human burial that this puppy was no wolf.

What are unarguably the skeletal remains of dogs have been found at the site of the hunter-gatherer summer camp at Starr Carr on the shore of what was a prehistoric lake – Lake Pickering – in Yorkshire. Starr Carr was settled just under 10 000 years ago and is a rich example of the culture of the human communities who settled across the broad north European plain which stretched uninterrupted from Russia to Wales after the last glaciers moved northwards. The residents of Starr Carr and similar camps throughout the region used bows and arrows, built canoes and developed axes

Unlike other animals, dogs were rapidly
brought into highly intimate contact with their human owners. By the time this resident
of Ein Mallaha on the coast of what is now Israel was buried about 12 000 years ago
they were regarded as fit companions for human journeys to eternity.

Hunting dogs like the pack
in the Masai Mara reservation of Kenya (*overleaf*) owe no human
allegiance. Many of the world's dogs live in a wild or semi-wild state.

and other wood-working tools to exploit the rich deciduous forests that had recently spread across Europe. Their way of life, which led them to live by lakes and streams, has given their culture the name 'Maglemosian', from the Danish words for 'great bog'.

Armed with bows and stone-tipped arrows (which may have had a range of up to 35 yards), the Maglemosians could more effectively prey on the wild cattle, pigs and elk that made up much of their diet. More accurate, and with a greater range than a spear, the bow and arrow allowed man to kill effectively at a distance. Largely because of their acute sense of smell, dogs were able to find the dead game. They were also able to protect it from other predators until the hunter arrived. Dogs could also seek and flush out game, and track wounded animals. As human weaponry continued to improve, men and dogs acted in an ever more lethal partnership and the Maglemosian hunting communities flourished – as did communities all over the world wherever man and dog worked together. Archaeological evidence shows that within the space of a few thousand years it had become so ubiquitous as to be commonplace for dogs to live alongside humans. By the time settled agricultural communities had become the dominant way of human life, dogs were established if not yet as man's best friend, certainly as his most useful one.

What the archaeological record cannot tell us is what these prehistoric dogs actually looked like. It is doubtful that any of them bore a specific resemblance to today's breeds. But it is clear that as soon as man had created the dog he set about improving it: breeding selectively to create animals that were suitable for specific tasks. Dogs to herd, to hunt, to watch. Darwin found it hard to believe that the hundreds of breeds of dogs that existed by his lifetime in the middle of the nineteenth century had all sprung from a single ancestor, the wolf.

That man has been able to transform the wolf in so many ways, from the lordly Great Dane to the tiny Chihuahua, demonstrates extraordinary ingenuity – and obsession. Why were so many, sometimes rather fanciful, dogs created? When and why was the dog transformed from a helper and companion to a mirror of our dreams as well as our needs? For the beginning of systematic breeding we have to look towards ancient Egypt in the years before 2000 BC.

It is hard to believe that the tiny papillon has much in common with either the bigger breeds of dog or its wild wolf ancestors.

CHAPTER THREE

MAKING FRIENDS

'Every dog has his day' and so does his master. The Pharaoh Antef II reigned for fifty-one years full of war and political adventure. Four thousand years ago his family, the XIth Dynasty, struggled against the rival kings of the Herakleopolitan Dynasty to extend their overlordship of central Egypt farther and farther north. Alas, Antef's own years of struggle resulted in only minor gains of territory. But he and his family were also culturally and socially ambitious. They energetically dispatched trading expeditions, exploited the mines and quarries of the neighbouring deserts, restored what were even then ancient monuments and built their own monuments as well. Just north of their capital city of Thebes, at El-Tarif, they constructed a huge necropolis: a city of the dead where Antef, his father and his son were all buried. Today Antef is remembered less for his imperial ambitions than for his dogs.

A few years after Antef's death, his son erected a stele or monumental stone slab praising the achievements of his father. This monument is one of the finest early depictions of different types of dogs. Sadly for the pharaoh, it is now more widely known as the 'Dog stele' than the 'Antef stele'. Three of his dogs are shown in profile, along with their names which we can roughly translate as 'Blackie' (alluding to colour), 'Gazelle' (alluding to speed) and 'Cauldron' (either referring to a huge appetite or,

The memorial stone for
Antef II, erected around 4000 years ago, is among the
earliest evidence of the creation of distinctly different
types of dogs through selective breeding.

maybe, to a character that was boiling over with ferocity). All three dogs wear heavy collars and are long-legged, powerful but relatively sleek-bodied types with curly tails. Two of them bear a close resemblance to greyhounds and the third vaguely resembles a basenji or Congo terrier.

Enthusiasts for a particular breed have an unhelpful, if understandable, tendency to immediately identify any early dog as their favourite's progenitor. It is, in fact, extremely difficult to do this because in many cases, right up to the Renaissance, dogs are depicted in an extremely stylized way. Just as we cannot expect the vast majority of Egyptian statues of pharaohs to be realistic portraits, we cannot expect sculptures and paintings of their dogs to be definitive studies of a specific animal or breed. Yes, there are dogs that look like greyhounds or mastiffs, but that really is as far as it goes. However, we can say that the Egyptians were able to create recognizable breeds, even though only a few of those breeds may have carried on into the present.

Fortunately for us, the Egyptians had fantastic powers of observation. They looked at their world with wonder and painted and carved prolifically. Thanks to an arid climate, much of what they did has been preserved for us. Largely because they believed that they could re-create the here and now in the afterlife, virtually every aspect of daily routine

Dogs pervaded the civilization of ancient Egypt. Fierce dogs were an indispensable part of any pharaonic hunting trip, as pictured on a gold fan (*previous page*) from Tutankhamun's tomb; and the mummified dog (*left*) is one of many thousands that show the extent to which dogs, and indeed many other animals, played a role in the spiritual life of the Egyptians.

was faithfully painted, modelled and sculpted in tombs. Until we reach relatively modern times, no civilization offers us such a detailed insight into the way life was lived in the past. For the first time, the Egyptians show us what real dogs in all their variety and all their usefulness were like.

We seem to have a mistaken idea that the ancient Egyptians were a death-obsessed, cat-worshipping nation. In fact, they were sophisticated, adventurous and full of *joie de vivre*. They sat on chairs that looked like and were built like ours, they wore linen clothes some of which would not look out of place in a modern resort, they drank beer and baked bread and gave dinner parties. But they were, of course, very different from us. Their well-being was based – sometimes precariously – on the ebb and flood of the Nile. There was plague, pestilence and war. Their spiritual life – which we will talk about later – was extraordinarily complex. Arbitrary gods had to be adored and propitiated.

The Egyptian attitude towards animals in many ways reflected the geography and economy of Egypt. The kingdom of the pharaohs was not exactly the land mass it appeared to be. It was instead a narrow strip of settlements hugging the Nile with vast deserts stretching out towards the horizons. It was, paradoxically, an island of water in a sea of sand. The great deserts were full of hyenas, gazelles and lions; the Nile was home to hippopotamuses and crocodiles. Egyptian skill at the domestication of animals meant that there was a workforce of donkeys who served as the principal beasts of burden, and herds of cattle and pigs for the slaughter. Horses were pharaonic and aristocratic, bred with great sophistication for both display and warfare. Monkeys were favourite domestic pets, as were cats.

The usefulness of the cat to the Egyptians was manifold. Cats ate mice and rats and protected valuable stores of grain. Their natural predatory instincts made them useful for flushing wild birds out of tall grass or thickets. Their beauty and unpredictability were also constant reminders of the spiritual world. The goddess Bastet had the head of a cat, and Sekhmet, goddess of war, the head of a lion.

In the fifth century B C Herodotus, the indefatigable traveller and historian of the ancient world, was enthralled and impressed by all things to do with Egypt. He remarked on the very large number of pets kept by its people and – some centuries after the Egyptian civilization had begun to decline – told his bemused Greek readers that, 'What happens when a house catches fire is most extraordinary: nobody takes the least trouble to put it out, for it is only the cats that matter: everyone stands in a row, a little distance from his neighbour, trying to protect the cat . . .

'All the inmates of a house where a cat has died a natural death shave their eyebrows,' Herodotus went on to observe. But 'when a dog dies they shave the whole body including the head.' So dogs were mourned at least as intensely as cats. Historians of the cat have made much of its role as a religious symbol in Egypt, and have often remarked upon the great number of mummified cats discovered at sacred sites. They may sometimes have failed to note that mummified beetles, snakes, mice, gazelles, baboons, crocodiles, ibises and dogs have also been found at these sites.

'The animals that do exist in the country,' Herodotus tells us, 'are all regarded as sacred. If I were to explain why they are consecrated to the several gods, I should be led to speak of religious matters, which I particularly shrink from mentioning.' Whether this was from discretion or mere bewilderment is hard to tell. But without getting too involved in the arcana of Egyptian religion, we can say that virtually every member of the whole pantheon of its gods – and a crowded pantheon it was, ranging from

Upper-class Egyptians
ground their cosmetics on highly decorated stone palettes.
This 5000-year-old example is decorated with vivid scenes of
hunting dogs cornering and exhausting prey.

Aker the earth god to Wadjet, a goddess of growth – had an animal form or familiar. As the semiologist Manfred Lurker points out, 'Only rarely was the animal regarded as the god itself ... The individual animal was only an earthly image ...' Dogs and their cousins – the wolf and the jackal – became the earthly images of a number of gods. Just as individual breeds are difficult to identify from art works, the dogs of the gods can sometimes only be broadly identified as canids. Most prominent among them are those of Anubis, god of the dead and embalming, Seth the fierce lord of the desert and Wepwawet, a battle god.

Apart from their religious role, dogs were most prized as hunting companions. The hunt was a highly organized and elaborate event and was largely a prerogative of the pharaoh and his great nobles who were assisted by professional huntsmen. One of the earliest representations of the dog as a hunting companion to man is on a pre-dynastic object dating from around 3300 BC, known as 'the hunter's palette'. A palette was a piece of stone used for grinding pigments, in this case the pigments that went into cosmetics. Ruling class Egyptians wore vast amounts of make-up – so much that they even considered it to be an integral part of clothing. Palettes were important objects and very often elaborately decorated. The hunter's palette is full of action: kilt-wearing hunters, armed with bows and arrows, spears and tomahawks, close in on a group of animals including lions, deer, gazelles, ostriches, rabbits and wolves. The hunters are helped by two dog-like animals with upturned ears and heavy, bushy tails. One of them is savaging a gazelle, the other a deer. The Egyptian hunting technique involved driving as many animals as possible into a restricted area, with the aid of dogs, and then slaughtering them. A wooden archery case dating from around 1800 BC, which probably belonged to a professional huntsman, has another scene of dogs at work. In this case they are harrying gazelle into a position where the huntsman can dispatch them with his flint-tipped arrows.

Anubis guards the treasury of Tutankhamun's tomb.

59

DOGS OF ANCIENT EGYPT

*To the Ancient Egyptians dogs were both mundane and divine.
As familiar, everyday animals some of them lived the low
life of despised strays while others enjoyed the high
life of a pharaoh's hunting companions. But dogs and dog-
like animals were frequently identified with the rich
and mysterious population
of Egyptian gods.*

LEFT *Anubis, the Egyptian lord of the
underworld, was usually shown as a human-
bodied god with a dog or dog-like head.*

RIGHT *This wooden mask
of Anubis, made sometime
between 1350 and 1115 BC,
has a hinged jaw and was
probably worn by a human priest.*

ABOVE *Before a dead man – in this case the royal scribe Hunefer who died around
1310 BC – could be admitted to the underworld, his heart was weighed against
the feather of truth in a ceremony supervised by the dog-headed Anubis
and judged by the god Osiris.*

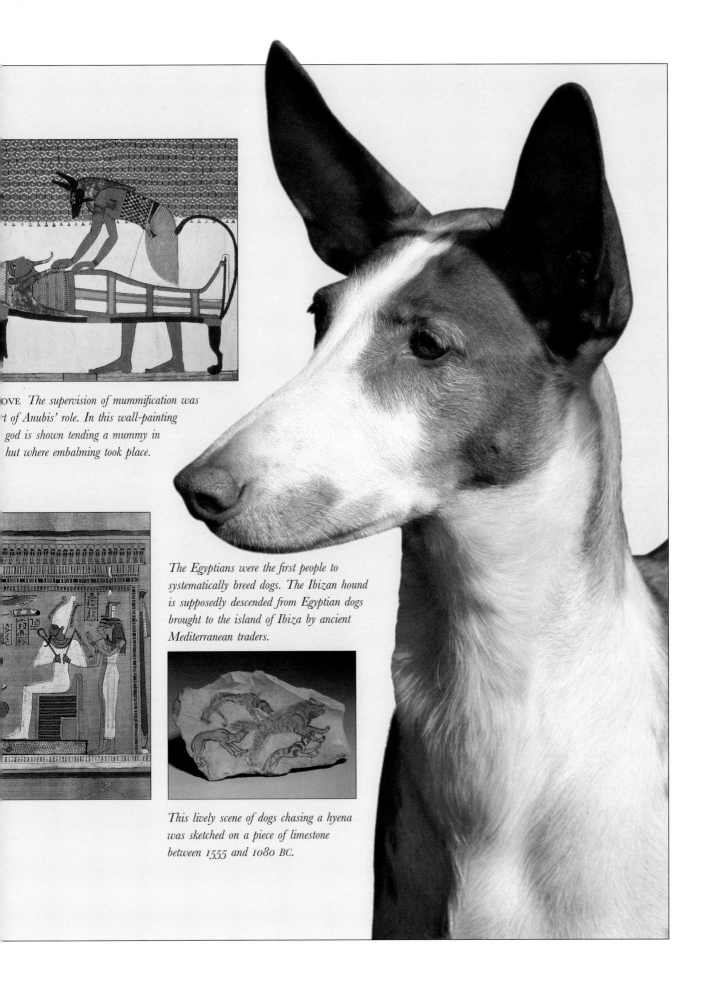

The supervision of mummification was
t of Anubis' role. In this wall-painting
god is shown tending a mummy in
hut where embalming took place.

The Egyptians were the first people to
systematically breed dogs. The Ibizan hound
is supposedly descended from Egyptian dogs
brought to the island of Ibiza by ancient
Mediterranean traders.

This lively scene of dogs chasing a hyena
was sketched on a piece of limestone
between 1555 and 1080 BC.

From earliest times the Egyptian habit of naming dogs tells us that good animals were highly prized and held in great affection. Cats, horses and even baboons were also given individual names, but dogs received them far more often than any other animal. Sometimes they referred to the dog's character, as we have seen with Antef's dogs. Sometimes they were human ones. And sometimes they praised a god or a king, as in the name 'Amun is valiant'.

Apart from their role as hunters, Egyptian dogs were used as watch-dogs, policemen and household pets. But while they were loved for their loyalty and valour, and indirectly worshipped for their association with the gods, they were also sometimes feared and despised. The pampered dogs who lived closely with their masters and were buried alongside them and praised in funerary inscriptions were selectively bred and, if not necessarily recognizable to us, were definite breeds. However, there was also an underclass of dog: homeless mongrels who may have continued to interbreed with wolves or jackals, who roamed the streets and fell victim to rabies and madness. It is tempting, although perhaps unhistorical, to look at the two classes of dogs as analogous to the two human classes of rulers and ruled. More importantly, the Egyptians seem to have established the long-lasting convention of pedigree dogs of known lineage for the aristocracy and mongrels for the populace.

They were also the first people to give tangible expression to some of the ambivalent feelings about dogs that still trouble us. They recognized that the animal that could be the earthly expression of a god could also be an object of terror, hatred and derision. As the Egyptologists Jack and Rosslyn Janssen have pointed out, the fear of rabies meant that dogs were companions for men rather than playmates for children. They also observed that they were frequently scorned for their servility and complaisance: defeated enemies were referred to as 'dogs' and officials in royal service compared themselves to them. None the less, the Egyptians lived in a spiritual world in which men, gods and beasts mingled freely and, unlike us, did not feel that they dominated the animal kingdom. Dogs, like cattle or donkeys, may have served man but they were very much felt to be fellow creatures.

Any number of Egyptian texts might be cited to underline this belief that men and animals were members of a community of living things. One story of the Creation, for example, tells us that the god Ptah – who was more or less the Egyptian creator god – is 'throughout every body and throughout every mouth of all gods, of all men, of all animals ...' Another text tells us: 'Well tended are men, the cattle of god', a metaphor with the fairly obvious implication that men should treat animals the way they expect god to treat man.

This attitude towards animals, and hence dogs, as being different but equal – and perhaps even touched by the gods – prevailed throughout most of the ancient Middle East for some thousands of years. Indeed, it is still found in some 'primitive' societies. You may also have noticed that it foreshadows some of today's fashionable ideas about 'green-ness' and ecological awareness.

THE GREEKS AND DOGS

The Greeks were intellectually restless and troublesome. They changed the rules and substantially redefined man's relationship to the animal world.

'Numberless are the world's wonders,' the Athenian dramatist Sophocles wrote in the fifth century BC, 'but none more wonderful than man.' And there you have it. The Greeks decisively moved away from the old ideas of man and nature in partnership. They put man at the centre of creation and firmly established the idea that he is nature's overlord. The consequences have been with us ever since. The Greeks invented science and philosophy and history as means to explain how the world worked. Their passion for questioning and cataloguing led them to examine every aspect of life.

The animal kingdom was, of course, subjected to intense scrutiny. Did animals have souls? How did they reproduce, digest, grow and alter? All these questions were asked by men of great intelligence and curiosity. In spite of the dog's demotion, as it were, from fellow creature to subservient creature, the Greeks recognized that it had qualities of intelligence as well as utility that raised it above the common run of animals. Perhaps they were most impressed by its ability to remember. Memory is one of the elements of consciousness that distinguishes human intelligence from that of animals. Without it, human life is adrift. The Greek exaltation of this faculty contributed to their invention of history which, after all, starts from the basis of collective memory. Herodotus, who is often called 'the Father of History', told his readers that his words were 'set down to preserve the memory of the past'. To the ancient Greeks the dog's ability to remember was almost human.

There are few more touching scenes of remembrance and loss in all of literature than the return of Odysseus as told by Homer in Book XVII of the *Odyssey* in *c.*800 BC.

The Greeks loved hunting and prized dogs most as hunting companions. Their vase paintings may have a cartoon-like simplicity, but for the first time in art the animals are full of life and vigour.

After fighting in the Trojan Wars and wandering the Mediterranean, Odysseus returns home to his kingdom of Ithaca after nineteen years. Disguised as a beggar, he is unrecognized until he comes across an elderly and neglected dog lying on a dung-heap. Homer tells how, when the dog heard Odysseus' voice, 'he did his best to wag his tail, nose down with flattened ears, having no strength to move nearer his master. And the man looked away wiping a salt tear from his cheek …' Odysseus had recognized his dog Argos, the young pup whom he had planned to train to hunt hare, wild goat and deer. Having waited a lifetime to see his master again, Argos dies. Later on, Odysseus is reunited with his wife Penelope and establishes his identity by describing the construction of their marital bed. Homer presented his readers with two proofs of Odysseus' identity which, together, seem to hint that a man's relationship with his dog is perhaps as intimate and intense as his relationship with his wife.

Certainly, dogs could be found in most upper-class Greek households. Although horses might have been a more striking symbol of aristocratic pride, as the historian Anthony Andrewes points out, dogs were the companions without whom the Greeks could not indulge their love of hunting. The group known as hounds – who find prey through their acute sense of sight and smell – was particularly prized. The Greeks favoured packs of small, beagle-like ones.

Some 300 or 400 years after Homer, we come to Aristotle whose drive to describe and explain the world led him to write at great length about everything from the sexuality of female elephants to the rules of classical drama. He did not speculate explicitly about the intelligence of the dog: we can only assume that he did not own one. But he did attempt to assign the dog a character. Some animals he wrote, 'are wild and treacherous as the wolf' or 'jealous and self-conceited as the peacock' or 'spirited and affectionate and fawning as the dog.' He also recognized that the dog has the ability to remember, and remarked upon the great difference that exists between those animals who have only perception and those higher ones who have both perception and memory.

For Aristotle, one of the principal functions of any organism was to reproduce itself and he wrote in some detail about the mating habits of dogs and other animals. Much of that writing now appears trivial, such as the observation that male dogs cock their legs to urinate while bitches usually squat. However, he also tells us that some breeds live to be fourteen or fifteen years, some live to be twenty and others die when they are ten. He writes that you can tell the age of a dog by examining its teeth, and that the female of the Laconian breed of dogs is cleverer than the male. He also describes one of the most famous breeds of antiquity: 'Of the Molossian breed of dogs, such as are employed in the chase are pretty much the same as those elsewhere; but the sheep-dogs of this breed are superior to the others in size and in the courage with which they face the attacks of wild animals.'

When we talk about ancient 'breeds' like the Molossian we really do need inverted commas. As you can tell from the passage just quoted, breed meant something very different in the ancient world. Aristotle talks about hounds and sheep-dogs both being members of the same breed – something that would be impossible today. There are, indeed, many references to this much-prized Molossian breed, all of them really rather misleading. We know that Molottia, a region of Epirus in north-western Greece, was famous for producing large, fierce dogs and that all dogs from this area were known as Molossian. It seems that coming from Molottia was a guarantee of high quality rather than the assurance that a dog would have a particular look. The Molossians are reputed to be descended from the Tibetan bulldog and to have fathered some modern dogs like the Saint Bernard. However, as we've seen with Egyptian breeds, it is all speculation. Even visual evidence can be misleading. A sculpture of the favourite dog of Alcibiades, the Athenian general, looks remarkably like a Newfoundland, but how likely is it that this early North American dog had an ancient Greek ancestor?

The myth of Actaeon, the hunter torn to death by his own pack of dogs, was a constant reminder to the Greeks that a wild animal lurked within the soul of even the most obedient hunting companion.

Dogs are common enough figures on painted Greek pottery, but more often than not they are schematic and sketchy rather than exact portraits. None the less, the pictures are full of life and vivacity: leads are strained, eyes flash, teeth are bared.

Both the Greeks and the Romans clearly recognized that dogs were inherently wild and made their fears most famously explicit in the popular myth of Actaeon and Diana. Actaeon was a well-born and skilful hunter. One day he accidentally caught a glimpse of the goddess Diana naked at her bath. Furious, she turned him into a stag and he was savaged to death by his own 'faithful' pack of hounds. The story was frequently retold, and painted in both ancient times and the Renaissance.

When the Roman poet Ovid recorded his version of the Actaeon myth he named and described thirty-two of the legendary hunter's dogs with great wit and affection. Among others were 'Whirlwind and Dingle from a she-wolf born ... And Hurricane untiring on the track ... And Barker shrill of tongue and Shag long haired ...' Imagine Actaeon's horror when 'A stag in shape, in mind he still was man' and was unable to prevent his beloved dogs from doing what he had trained them so well to do.

> He groans a noise twixt deer and man,
>> And fills with cries of pain the well remembered hills;
> And kneels within the pitiless ring to raise,
>> Instead of arms a mute beseeching gaze.

In Actaeon's death we witness what happens when the thin line between civilization and savagery is broken and the beast within our best friend runs wild. As a story of man murdered by his own creation it has all the dread and drama of Frankenstein.

THE ROMANS AND DOGS

I have always disliked the view that the Romans were the ruthless, but dull, consolidators of Greek inventiveness. Like the Greeks they hunted with dogs, painted and carved them and wrote about them. But they seem to me, at any rate, to have introduced a greater warmth into the relationship between man and dog. Dogs appear to have been fully fledged members of Roman households, sleeping indoors and playing with the children. No household was complete without one. Even the Lares, the gods who were believed to look after domestic property, were usually portrayed either wearing dog-skins or accompanied by dogs.

A very beautiful and charming late Roman terracotta sculpture, *The Bordeaux Lovers*, depicts a naked man and woman locked in a lusty embrace under the bedclothes while a small dog sleeps peacefully at the foot of the bed. In the heat of his master's and mistress's passion he dreams of rabbits. I cannot think of any other work of art – painting or sculpture – that so joyfully shows the easy intimacy that can develop between humans and dogs.

The Roman towns and countryside were full of dogs. They dash through Roman landscapes on wall-paintings, and hunt boar and hare in mosaic floors found across the Empire from Syria to England. And, of course, there are the most stunning of any dog images from antiquity – the *Cave canem* ('Beware of the dog') mosaics found in front of so many Roman houses. My own favourite is the celebrated one from the House of the Poet in Pompeii. A rough-coated dog, teeth bared, tail up, front paws flattened, ears pricked, full of vigilance and expectation, pulls at his chain. These strong and simple images have inspired an unusual amount of theorizing. One writer

suggests that 'Beware of the dog' means 'Please don't step on the family lap-dog'. Another hints that it is not a warning at all, just a notice that the family keeps a dog. Burglary and theft were common enough in Roman towns and cities, though, to justify the obvious explanation that, however gentle and loving dogs may have been in the family circle, these mosaics were meant to portray them as fierce deterrents to any intruder. Indeed, the Romans, who could themselves be hard and aggressive, fully appreciated and manipulated their dogs' potential for violence. Big, fierce dogs –

Roman dogs were often
kept as burglar alarms and the fact was announced
in mosaic pavements like this one from Pompeii (*above*). But they
were also intimate members of the household. In a Gallo-Roman
earthenware (*left*) a pet dog sleeps soundly while his
owners make love.

sometimes even dressed in armour – were important members of the legions and the Romans regarded breeds like mastiffs as being among Britain's most noteworthy exports. In the arenas of Roman cities dogs attacked and killed prisoners-of-war, slaves and religious dissenters as part of a day's entertainment for the crowds. Nevertheless, the role of the dog in Roman life was mostly benign.

The Romans fully developed the dog's ability to to be bred in a confounding range of shapes and sizes, from the little lap-dogs of aristocratic ladies that so irritated Julius Caesar to the huge war-dogs of the legions. Both the Egyptians and the Greeks had imported dogs, but the Romans developed a large-scale international trade in them.

The soldier statesman and scientist Pliny the Elder, who died at Pompeii when he insisted on carefully, perhaps I should say too carefully, observing the eruption of Vesuvius in AD 79, wrote in his great *Natural History*: 'Many of our domesticated animals are worth learning about, and the most faithful to man, bar none, are the dog and the horse ... Only dogs know their master and recognize a stranger if he arrives unexpectedly. They alone recognize their own names and the voices of members of the family. Dogs remember the way to places, however far away and no animal has a better memory except man ... Every day of our lives we find very many other qualities in dogs ...' Here we have the voice of one of the most intelligent and active men of the Roman world expressing an admiration and love of dogs which speaks directly to us.

That admiration and love also produced beautifully observed and moving works of art like the so-called Townley greyhounds with their stunning conjunction of anatomical correctness and psychological accuracy. They adorned an aristocratic villa near Rome and are deft, impressive and, of course, very beautiful. As beautiful, in fact, as real dogs. But an altogether more modest sculpture – also of a hound – goes straight to my heart because it is so accurately observed and so full of real empathy.

By Roman times
there were some breeds at least that seem familiar
to us. Even after nearly 2000 years the so-called
Townley greyhounds look well muscled and
eager to run.

It is a 7.5 centimetre (3 inch) long bronze and was found at a provincial temple in England. The hound's coat is beautifully modelled and he sits comfortably, his front legs stretched out. But the artist has caught him in that exact moment between repose and action, with his head quickly turned around as if in response to his master's footstep. This unpretentious work brings us close to the everyday life of the Romans

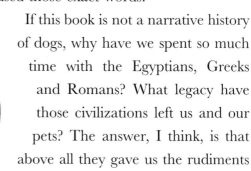

and their dogs. The Romans certainly created the belief that the dog was 'man's best friend' even if they never used those exact words.

If this book is not a narrative history of dogs, why have we spent so much time with the Egyptians, Greeks and Romans? What legacy have those civilizations left us and our pets? The answer, I think, is that above all they gave us the rudiments

of the cosy, domestic relationship with dogs that many of us enjoy today. Although the Greeks and the Romans tried to demystify our attitude towards dogs, their attempts at a rational, scientific description of dogs and their abilities did nothing to diminish the animal's mystique. Indeed, its astonishing powers and nearly human character continued to endow it with spiritual and psychic significance.

Pathfinder and hunter without equal, faithful until death and beyond, who could be a better friend for man in this world or the next?

This scene from a
piece of Romano-British pottery (*above*) epitomizes
the speed and strength of well-bred hunting dogs.

This little, provincial Roman
bronze of a reclining hound (*left*) was found at a temple in England.
Modest and unassuming, it is marvellously observed and full of
the love and intimacy that the Romans felt for their dogs.

·CHAPTER FOUR·

DOGS AND GOD

'Man is the God of the dog whose ... whole soul is wrapped up in his God!' wrote the eighteenth-century Scottish poet Robert Burns. 'All the powers and faculties of his nature are devoted to his service! And these powers and faculties are ennobled by the intercourse. Divines tell us that it just ought to be so with the Christian, but the dog puts the Christian to shame.' Man *is* the God of the dog, but affairs between man's god and the dog have rarely been straightforward. Religions have venerated dogs and held them in contempt; they have made them symbols of divinity and corruption, virtue and wickedness.

Followers of three of the great monotheistic religions – Judaism, Christianity and Islam – have sometimes had uneasy relationships with man's best friend. A fourth religion – Zoroastrianism – treats dogs with astonishing reverence. From six hundred years before Christ until seven hundred years after, it was the state religion of the old Persian empires. Today, many of the surviving Zoroastrians live in India where they are known as Parsees.

'The dog has eight characters,' their sacred scriptures tell us. 'One like a priest, one like a warrior, one like a husbandman, one like a singer, one like a thief, one like a wild beast, one like a courtesan, one like a child.' We are then told, with remarkable accuracy and poetry, about each of these characters. The dog is like a child, for example, because, 'He loves sleep like a child, he is fawning like a child, he cries often

Dogs have been powerful religious symbols from ancient times. In this sixteenth-century painting dogs play the part of clergy in a fiercely anti-Catholic allegory.

like a child, he runs forward like a child.' Zoroastrian writings are full of detailed instructions about the treatment of dogs and severe punishments for those who transgress them. Whoever wounds a cattle-dog is to receive 800 blows with a horse goad; whoever wounds a young dog is to receive 500 blows, and so on.

As well as giving dogs special consideration and protection, the Zoroastrians integrated them into some of their most important religious ceremonies and rites of passage. Dead bodies, for example, are still subjected to the practice of *sag did*, which literally means 'dog view'. A dog is brought alongside a body, first to determine that there are absolutely no signs of life, and second to drive away the corpse demoness who embodies death and decay. Dogs also take part in the elaborate purification rituals that are such a key part of the religion. Believers touch one with their left hand during each step in a series of complex ablutions involving bulls, urine and water. Furthermore, dogs are reputedly able to slay demons in the night.

Why do the Zoroastrians raise dogs to such a high status? Before I answer that question, I ought to say that simple functional or utilitarian explanations for religious beliefs or practices have to be viewed with a degree of scepticism. Reason and belief are not always unruffled bedfellows. But if we look at the antecedents of the Zoroastrians we can see that their lives depended on dogs. The early Indo-Iranians were a pastoral people who nurtured their herds and flocks in the mountain ranges around the Hindu Kush in central Asia, an area that remains harsh and forbidding even today. As a people without horses they relied on dogs to control and protect the herds which gave them milk, meat and raw materials. It was a marginal and spartan existence, ensured only by the talent and fidelity of dogs.

DOGS IN THE MIDDLE EAST

These Indo-Iranians flourished and spread into the more fertile lands of Persia but they never forgot their debt. They believed that Ahura Mazda, 'the Wise Lord', a Zoroastrian name for God, created dogs 'with keen scent and sharp teeth … faithful to men as a protection to the fold.' Their holy writings go on to tell us that without them there could be no civilization, 'For the dwellings would not stand fast on the earth … if there were not dogs which pertain to the cattle and the village.'

Even though all of creation is prized by Muslims because 'Allah does not create anything in which there is not a trace of his wisdom,' dogs have at times been held in particularly low esteem by Middle Eastern cultures, who have believed them to be impure both through their licks and their mere presence. Some Zoroastrian commentators think that any disdain for dogs may be a direct result of the Muslim conquest of Zoroastrian Persia in the seventh century AD. Mary Boyce, a historian of Zoroastrianism, wrote that early Islam did not advocate unkindness towards dogs although there was 'Muslim hostility to the dog as an unclean animal, and this it seems was deliberately fostered in Iran because of the remarkable Zoroastrian respect for dogs.' Boyce further feels that mistreating dogs 'was a distinctive outward sign of true conversion'. Doing the opposite of one's religious rivals is a persistent habit. The persecution of Jews in fifteenth-century Spain, for example, was accompanied by the development of highly elaborate pig-butchering and curing ceremonies designed to show enthusiasm for a food that was taboo to Jews

However, any idea that Middle Eastern religion and culture has always been implacably disdainful of dogs is a rather coarse over-simplification of a shifting and sophisticated relationship. Persian painting of the fifteenth and sixteenth centuries is full of glamorous and affectionate portrayals of hunting hounds like the Saluki.

There is also a rich Arabic dog literature. One of the first masters of Arabic prose, the prolific ninth-century scholar Al Djahiz, wrote about dogs with acute observation and admiration in a manner reminiscent of Aristotle whose work he greatly admired. In his famous bestiary, he describes the most popular breeds of the Islamic world: the Saluki, the Kurdish sheep-dog and one that is a cross between the two.

The brilliantly titled *Book of The Superiority of Dogs over many of Those who wear Clothes* is a tenth-century panegyric to the canine. 'Somebody criticizing dogs said "People sleep at night a time God has appointed for repose,"' its author Ibn al-Marzuban relates, before explaining that, 'Dogs stay awake at night simply because it is a time when thieves are abroad; many walls are scaled or penetrated and robbery is rife, carried out by those who, when they come to someone's house are content with nothing less than killing, committing evil and plundering property. Dogs guard against such happenings and wake up the master of the house.'

The Arabic love of falconry, which persists in the contemporary Middle East, encouraged the breeding and acquisition of bird-dogs which would flush small game out into the open where it could be attacked by trained birds of prey. Arabic princes imported pointers from Europe at fabulous expense. Arabic literature also mentions

Fast and glamorous, Salukis (*above*)
hunt by sight rather than scent and were eagerly bred and luxuriously treated by medieval
Middle Eastern and Asiatic princes. The late seventeenth-century Mogul miniature (*right*) shows
the Indian emperor Akbar the Great hunting with his imperial hounds – Saluki
who had the speed to hunt members of the antelope family like the black buck seen here.

diverse breeds like 'the stocky dog' – a Pomeranian type – and the sini, which literally means 'Chinese' and probably refers to a Pekingese or pug. The Arabic love of hunting and the development of a highly cultured court life both provided opportunities for the skilful breeding and keeping of dogs.

None the less, the dog has also been viewed in the Arabic world as an unclean animal and even today there are people who believe that anything it licks or touches is rendered impure, and that no angel will enter a house in which a dog is present. Where do the roots of this antipathy lie? Surely there must be more to it than just a desire to torment the dog-loving Zoroastrians.

We have to go back to the historical condition of dogs throughout the Middle East. We mentioned that while the Egyptians loved the dogs that were their companions and helpers, they also feared and hated the 'underclass' of hostile and sometimes rabid strays that roamed the streets. These pariah dogs plagued the Middle East for centuries. As late as the nineteenth century Muhammad Ali, viceroy of Egypt, was able to round up enough pariah dogs to fill a substantial ship which was then sunk with the hapless animals on board. To this day, the word 'dog' is particularly insulting to speakers of Middle Eastern languages.

Many of the conditions that coloured Arabic thinking about dogs had affected Jewish attitudes to them some centuries before. The Old Testament is full of hostile and derogatory references. Dogs roamed around the villages of ancient Israel scavenging, as in Exodus: 'You are not to eat the flesh of anything killed by beasts in the open country; you are to throw it to the dogs'; disturbing the peace, as in Psalms: 'They come out at nightfall snarling like dogs as they prowl about the city'; and filthy and violent, as in Proverbs: 'A fool who repeats his folly is like a dog returning to his vomit' and 'Like someone who seizes a stray cur by the ears is he who meddles in a quarrel not his own'. It is not until we reach the Apocryphal book of Tobit that the Jewish scriptures have a good word for dogs. As Tobias searches for a cure for his father Tobit's blindness, his dog is a faithful and constant companion on his wanderings:

The story of Tobit is one of the only kindly Old Testament references to dogs. In this fifteenth-century painting by a follower of Verrocchio, Tobias is accompanied on his journey by an angel and an eager, white ball of fluff of a dog (*bottom left*).

Cosimo Rosselli placed
a combative cat and dog as a humorous footnote to this
Last Supper in the Sistine Chapel, adding a lighthearted
touch to one of the great themes of Christian art.

Other saints – Dominic, Roch, Eustace, Hubert and Bernard of Aosta – have had dogs as their emblems. Hubert, a keen huntsman and eighth-century archbishop of Liège, was made the patron saint of dogs, and the rather less well known Sithney, a Breton/Cornish saint, became identified as the patron of mad ones. A Breton folk-tale tells us that when God asked Sithney to be the patron saint of girls he answered that he would prefer to be in charge of mad dogs rather than deal with the problems girls would give him. The St Christopher and the St Sithney stories have expropriated Freud's sexually 'shameless' dog and turned him into a badge of at best chastity and at worst misogyny. Christopher would rather look like a dog than be bothered by women; Sithney would rather care for mad dogs than deal with women.

The Christian Church also turned the dog's fidelity and tenacity into religious virtues. The punning nickname for the Dominican order of monks was *domini canes*

(dogs of god). In a thirteenth-century collection of religious stories, the *Gesta Romanorum*, priests are exhorted to emulate the watchfulness, the fidelity, the keen nose and the healing lick of dogs.

DOGS AS HEALERS

The idea that a dog's lick can heal reverberates over the centuries, through paganism and Christianity. To anyone who does not love dogs, and indeed to some who do, being licked by one is a sticky, dirty and repulsive experience. But a dog's lick has been long and widely reputed to have miraculous healing powers that are even deserving of a mention in the New Testament. Luke tells us that as Lazarus lay dying in front of the rich man's gate dogs would come and lick his sores. In the legend of Saint Roch, the plague-stricken hermit was nursed back to health by the ministrations of his dog. The village of San Rocco (Roch's Italian name) in Liguria still celebrates his feast day with a service of blessing and a public awards ceremony for heroic dogs.

Mythology frequently associates dogs with the healing arts. Gula, the ancient Babylonian goddess of healing, was often accompanied by them and one of her temples was known as the Dog House. In Armenian mythology dog-like spirits, known as the Aralez, licked the wounds of warriors killed in battle as a prelude to resurrection.

Eustace (*left*) is among the many Christian saints associated with dogs. A pagan hunter, he converted when he faced a stag with a cross between its antlers. This 1501 engraving is by Albrecht Dürer.

When the hermit Saint Roch or Rocco (*right*) was struck down by the plague a dog fed and nursed him back to health: he became the patron saint of dogs.

Archaeologists excavating
the ancient trade centre of Ashkelon on the Mediterranean coast found
hundreds of dogs that had been carefully buried over 2000 years ago.
The dogs may have been associated with an ancient healing cult.

Depictions of Asclepius, physician among the Greek gods, frequently show him with dogs and his shrine at Epidaurus had a resident population of sacred ones.

Although the dog's lick is no longer thought to be curative, dogs are used therapeutically. Their calming effect is particularly useful in the treatment of heart-attack victims and sufferers from high blood pressure. And a considerable mass of actuarial evidence supports the view that people who own dogs live longer. But the most spectacular example of the dog as a medical help to man comes from the ruined city of Ashkelon on the south-western coast of Israel.

The city was a seaport of some significance from the time of the Ancient Egyptians right up to the start of the Crusades in the eleventh century. A succession of Mediterranean peoples lived there – Canaanites, Phoenicians, Philistines, Greeks and

Persians – and it exported onions throughout the Roman world. (Scallion, the common American word for a spring onion, derives from Ashkelon.) In the late 1980s Lawrence Stager, an American archaeologist, was excavating warehouses there when he made an astonishing discovery: 'Suddenly we encountered not a building, but a few dogs.' Over the following seasons more and more dogs were found. 'It became quite a mystery,' Stager relates, 'why suddenly this tremendous number of dogs were concentrated in areas along the sea and over in another square.' He and his team found hundreds of dogs, ranging from puppies to mature animals, all of which had been carefully buried some time in the fifth century BC. The archaeologists believe that they had 'roamed about the sacred precincts and participated in the healing rituals' associated with a Phoenician healing cult.

DOG-HEADED HUMANS AND FERAL CHILDREN

Christopher may be Christianity's only dog-headed saint, but dog-headed humans are mentioned in travel writings that date back to the classical world. In the first century AD, for example, the Greek geographer Strabo told of the Ethiopian race of Cynamolgi who had the heads of dogs and barked at each other. Such beliefs persisted into the Middle Ages. Marco Polo thought that the Andaman Islands in the Bay of Bengal were populated by men with dogs' heads. There is an endless fascination with the idea that the attributes of men and dogs can mingle to produce sometimes divine, sometimes merely curious, creatures. The whole practice of 'cyanthropy', or the transformation of a man into a dog, is the stuff of a thousand folk-tales and legends.

The fancy that the two can mix grows out of our feeling that dogs are almost human – a feeling that also gives rise to the frequently expressed belief that dogs can nurture humans. A number of tabloid headlines from around the world – Puppy Boy Cocked His Leg Like A Dog, Wolf Boy Found In India – testify to the popularity of the idea of the feral child.

In *The Jungle Book*, Rudyard Kipling gave the feral child myth its most poetic expression in the story of 'Mowgli's Brothers': ' "How little! How naked, and – how bold!" said Mother Wolf softly. The baby was pushing his way between the cubs to get close to the warm hide. "Ahai! He is taking his meal with the others. And so this is a man's cub. Now was there ever a wolf that could boast of a man's cub among her children?" ' Occasionally human infants have been, in a manner of speaking, 'raised'

DOG-HEADED BEINGS

There is a persistent fantasy in cultures and religions all over the world that dogs and humans might create a breed that is half man and half dog. Travel writers in the classical world reported remote countries where tribes of dog-headed humans lived.

BELOW
An American Indian medicine man performs a ritual over a dying man in this painting by George Catlin (1794–1872). He wears a dog-skin, possibly hinting at the dog's ability to guide us – in this case into the next world.

ABOVE & RIGHT *The contemporary Belgian artist Thierry Poncelet paints dogs' heads on the human bodies of nineteenth-century portraits, using the animals to reflect human ideas about class and status.*

BELOW *With the head of a dog or jackal on a human body, Anubis, god of the underworld, is one of the most instantly recognizable of Egyptian deities.*

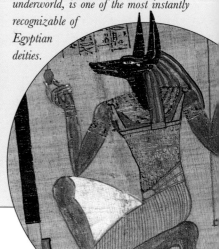

ABOVE *This illustration from a medieval manuscript describing the 'wonders' of Marco Polo, shows the rather tame daily activities of a group of 'dog-headed monsters of the East'.*

RIGHT *In some early Christian traditions Saint Christopher was depicted with a dog's head.*

by dogs, but the belief that canids could care for a human baby from infancy has been discredited.

What is surprising is the number of cultures that have ascribed their origins to some sort of canid nursemaid. The Romans were entirely prepared to accept that their ancestors, the twins Romulus and Remus, were suckled by a she-wolf, and the wolf and twins became the symbol of Rome. Various peoples of East and South-East Asia believe that they are descended from the marriage between a princess and a dog. Dogs are also important in the origin myths of other cultures. They were believed to

have taught the Mayas of Central America how to plant corn and the Chinese to grow rice. The Bambuti pygmies believe dogs taught them how to hunt and the Shoshone Indians of North America credit them with the gift of fire. Certain Aboriginal groups of the Australian desert believe that in 'dreamtime' – the mythic creation period of the world – a dingo was among their ancestors.

Why would people as different as the ancient Romans and the Aboriginals want

The idea that humans
could be raised by canids is almost universal. In *The
Jungle Book* Rudyard Kipling had the human cub 'Mowgli'
(*opposite*) raised by wolves; the Romans may have felt that their mythic
ancestors Romulus and Remus (*above*) imbibed great power
from their lupine foster mother's milk.

Dingoes roam the slopes
of Ayers Rock in Australia's Northwest Territory (*above*). In the difficult
for us to understand concept of 'dreamtime', some native Australians
identify the dingo as their ancestor. These Pintubi tribesmen (*right*)
have tamed dingoes for use as hunting dogs, but the animals will not
necessarily become domesticated. Dingoes drift in and out of Aboriginal
society and occupy a place halfway between the wild
and the domesticated state. They may be more like the first
dogs than any others in the world.

to credit canids with such a role in their history? A possible answer is that dogs are widely, if unconsciously, recognized as somehow occupying the shadowy ground between man and nature, magic and logic. Men feel they understand dogs, and that dogs may provide a link to powerful natural forces beyond man's understanding. An ancestral link with them may be felt to confer some sort of natural power on a people.

DOGS AND THE AFTERLIFE

Like the ancestor-dog, the association of dogs with death and the afterlife is found in an astounding variety of cultures. Why do death and dogs go together so often? One reason may be the sad fact of the dog's relatively short life span. We see its whole life, from infancy to old age and death, so the presence of our best friend is sometimes a *memento mori*. If the less than a score of years that it survives shows us that life ought to be lived with joy and intensity, it is also a constant reminder that death must ultimately be faced.

Perhaps that is why the howling of dogs is regarded as a harbinger of death among so many peoples throughout the world. In Icelandic mythology, when the dog Garm stands by the mouth of his lair and barks it will be the signal for Ragnarok – the cataclysmic death of the world.

In the Greek underworld Cerberus, the multi-headed hound of hell, both wagged his tale in welcome and mercilessly prevented anyone from escaping. The Chukchis

The Greeks believed that
the many-headed dog Cerberus, here depicted in a medieval
bestiary, stood guard over the entrance to Hades.

of Siberia believed that the death demon Ke'lets hunted men with the aid of a hound. However, the role of dogs in the afterlife has generally been altogether more benign. Men have wanted to associate them with life after death because they know that their fidelity, their love and their navigational skill will make the journey into the next life tolerable. Xolotl, the dog-headed god of the Incas who helps the dead across the nine-fold stream into the underworld, is just one example out of many.

The whole issue of whether dogs themselves may enjoy a life after death is impossibly speculative and awash with sentiment. Of course, even the most obdurate materialists (who believe that man and dog alike are complex machines) may believe in an afterlife. But most theories are based on a belief in the existence of the soul as an immaterial seat of thoughts, feelings and emotions. Do lobsters, ladybirds or antelopes have souls? It all depends on your religion or beliefs. Do dogs have souls? Most people who own one would hope so, and few wish to be separated from their dogs for ever. How could man be arrogant enough to believe that heaven and hell are his alone? 'Shall we, because we walk on our hind feet, assume to ourselves only the privilege of imperishability?' asked the English novelist George Eliot. 'Shall we,

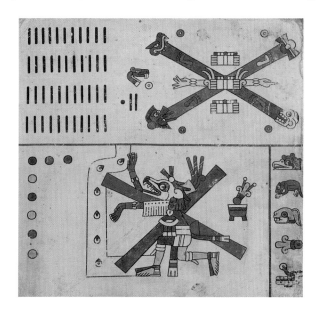

The dog-headed Aztec deity Xolotl greeted believers after death and guided them on their journey to the underworld.

who are even as they though we wag our tongues and not our tails, demand a special Providence and a selfish salvation?'

Martin Luther attempted to answer the unanswerable when he wrote: 'Be comforted little dog, thou too in the Resurrection, shall have a golden tail.' For thousands of years, men have asked or ordered their dogs to do work that has been dirty, dangerous and difficult. Is Luther's 'golden tail' a great enough reward for the bravery, the suffering and the ingenuity of our best friends?

CHAPTER FIVE

THE DOGS OF WORK

'**N**ever were dogs or men more faithful than those poor brutes', wrote Admiral Robert Peary in tribute to the dogs who helped him reach the North Pole in 1910. 'Day after day they struggled back across that awful frozen desert, fighting for their lives and ours. Day after day they worked 'til the last ounce of strength was gone from them, and then they fell dead in their tracks without a sound ...'

Towards the end of the nineteenth century the industrialized nations were seized by a collective mania to conquer the last places on earth: the Arctic and Antarctic. This heroic era of polar exploration, which ended with Peary triumphant in the north and Amundsen in the south, was marked by extremes of bravery and deprivation which reached mythic proportions. It was the greatest joint achievement of men and dogs in history; and without dogs it could not have happened when or how it did.

The huskies, Malemutes, laikas and Samoyeds of the circumpolar regions are superbly adapted for life and work in their harsh and unforgiving environment. They belong to a group of dogs known as 'spitz', the German word for pointed, which describes their prominent wolf-like muzzles. Although some spitz, like the Pomeranian, are often seen as domestic pets, these compact, muscular, thick-coated dogs have been

Huskies (*right* and *overleaf*)
pull heavy loads over long distances – the explorer Roald Amundsen was
awestruck by his dogs' ability to cover nearly twenty miles a day over hilly terrain.
Their thick coats protect them against even the most extreme polar temperatures.

the motive force of Arctic life for centuries, habitually traversing vast, freezing, sparsely populated lands. As the European economy encroached on the Arctic regions, the native peoples added the trade in furs to their normal occupations of hunting and fishing. This way of life involved even more travelling and it has been estimated that some groups were on the move, by dogsled, for as much as nine months in a year. The result was the development of a phenomenal ability to travel efficiently in hostile conditions, as well as an intimacy between dogs and people unparalleled in other parts of the world.

In the 1970s an American anthropologist, Joel Savishinsky, conducted extensive fieldwork among the Hare Indians in the Northwest Territories of Canada and found that dogs played a major part in their emotional life. Savishinsky was surprised to find that these emotionally reserved people would publicly lavish affection only on infants and puppies. Whereas we often give our dogs human names, the Hare Indians sometimes name people after their favourite dogs. Small children are given pups to raise – in Savishinsky's phrase 'the child is father to the dog' – and, between the ages of five and ten, are given 'in miniature a complete dogsled outfit to play and experiment with while they are gaining experience in handling the dogs themselves.' At about six months the young dogs are considered old enough to take their place in a team of adults and are harnessed up and left to learn from experience through what Savishinsky describes as 'a long, hazardous and painful process'. The life of the pampered pup is abruptly transformed as it faces 'new levels of discipline, authority, strenuous work and dominance competition within the adult team.' Outsiders have marvelled, and still marvel, at the result. When you watch an experienced team of man and dogs racing across a snowy landscape, instantly reacting to every nuance of the terrain, you see a rhythmical combination of power and beauty that turns transport into art.

In the early twentieth century the American novelist Jack London became the Homer of the husky with his acute poetic descriptions of these dogs at work: 'Down the frozen waterway toiled a string of wolfish dogs. Their bristly fur was rimmed with frost. Their breath froze in the air as it left their mouths, spouting forth in spumes of vapour that settled upon the hair of their bodies and formed into crystals of frost.'

However, not everyone has been so impressed with these 'wolfish dogs'. Addressing a geographical conference in Berlin in 1899, Sir Clements Markham, secretary of the Royal Geographical Society, declared that, 'In recent times much reliance has been placed upon dogs for Arctic travelling. Yet nothing has been done with them to be compared with what men have achieved without dogs.' To Sir Clements and his disciples, who included the doomed Robert Falcon Scott, dogs were unreliable, irrational and aboriginal. To men like Sir Clements, exploration was about progress and the white man's triumph, not about observing and adapting 'native' methods.

One expert who would have disagreed with him was the Norwegian explorer Fridtjof Nansen who had been the first European to successfully study the problems of Arctic transport. For many years visitors to the north had been fascinated by the sledges used by its native peoples, especially by the light but sturdy Inuit sledge, the komatik. Attempts to modernize it were fruitless as rigid, nailed joints and heavy, iron runners completely changed its character and usefulness. Preparing for his successful crossing of the Greenland ice fields in 1888, Nansen went back to first principles and designed a modified komatik which retained the ash frame and leather bindings of the original Inuit model. Flexible, manoeuvrable and almost crash-resistant, the Nansen sledge became the polar means of transport for nearly a hundred years. Ironically, when Nansen himself first used the new design he was unable to get any dogs and the sledges had to be manhauled.

The Nansen 'school' of exploration was committed to dogs and sledges for practical and psychological reasons. Otto Sverdrup, a veteran explorer and dog driver, pointed out that it was the dogs 'who give a polar journey its character: without them travel would indeed be grim.' The sledge dogs were more than just the means to an end. The writer Roland Huntford sums it up well: 'The relationship between dog and driver had to be that between equals; a dog was not a horse, he was a partner, not a beast of burden. And the Eskimo dog was a comfort in the polar wastes. He was a companion, amusing, touching, exasperating, but always diverting.'

DOGS IN THE ANTARCTIC

From the end of the nineteenth century to the eve of the First World War, the exploration of the Antarctic and the drive to reach the South Pole aroused the energy and imagination of the world. From a great number of talented and driven men two great rivals – Robert Falcon Scott and Roald Amundsen – emerged to engage in what turned out to be a tragic and deadly struggle. Their race to the pole became a twentieth-century myth with the chivalric Scott and his companions dying a noble death in the footsteps of the efficient and mundane Norwegian. Scott's failure was popularly regarded as a greater triumph than Amundsen's success.

In *Scott and Amundsen*, which generated amazing rancour and controversy when it was first published, Roland Huntford neatly demolishes the Scott myth. This is not the place to enter the greater depths of the controversy about Scott's personality or competence, but it seems to me pretty obvious that his death and Amundsen's triumph were both almost entirely the result of their different approaches to the use of dogs. We know that Scott insisted – possibly with the best and most idealistic motives – on the use of ponies and motorized sledges as well as dogs. The sledges broke down, the ponies froze to death in their own sweat and the dogs, upon whom all reliance was ultimately placed, were neither good enough, plentiful enough nor handled with sufficient skill. Scott's companion Captain Oates summed it up bitterly: '3 motors at

Samson (*above*), one of the
prized dogs on Shackleton's *Endurance* expedition of 1914–1916, poses in front
of his dogloo – a kennel built from snow and ice – with all the panache of any polar
hero. Ernest Joyce (*right*), the hard-drinking chief of dogs on Shackleton's British
Antarctic Expedition, poses proudly with huskie pups born in the spring of 1908.

£1000 each, 19 ponies at £6 each, 32 dogs at 30/- each. If Scott fails to get to the pole he jolly well deserves it.' Amundsen relied entirely on dogs.

Ernest Shackleton gives us an insightful look at an explorer's dogs in *South*, the memoirs of his polar expeditions published in 1919. The names are an impressive mixture of tributes to the heroes of antiquity (Ulysses, Hercules, Samson), the dogs' own characters (Snapper, Painful, Satan) and the virtues of English public schools (Upton, Rugby). In a particularly splendid photograph, Samson poses imperiously in front of a snow-covered hut or 'dogloo', as handsome and confident as the most romantic polar hero. Although by no means Shackleton's biggest dog, he astonished the explorer by 'starting off at a smart pace with a sledge carrying 200 pounds of blubber *and* a driver.'

With almost the singular exception of Scott – 'Bit by bit I am losing all faith in the dogs ... I am afraid we can place but little reliance on our dog teams,' he wrote – the explorers of the poles were awestruck by their dogs' strength and abilities. Here is what Amundsen, on his way to the South Pole, had to say in his unemotional way: 'This day's work – nineteen and a quarter miles with an ascent of 5750 feet – gives us some idea of what can be performed by dogs in good training. Our sledges still had what might be considered heavy loads; it seems superfluous to give the animals any other testimonial than the bare fact.'

A less praiseworthy fact was that these splendid dogs, having worked their hearts out for their masters, were put down when their labour was no longer required.

Amundsen describes the occasion when twenty-four of the Norwegian expedition's dogs had to be shot. He was on mess duty at the primus stove, busily stirring pemmican and trying to take his mind off the grim executions to come. 'There went the first shot – I am not a nervous man, but I must admit that I gave a start. Shot now followed upon shot – they had an uncanny sound over the great plain. A trusty servant lost his life each time.' The dead dogs were butchered and fed to fellow dogs and former masters alike. Amundsen and his men may have bitterly called that particular camp 'the Butcher's Shop', but within twenty-four hours they ate their 'trusty servants' with little remorse.

Dogs had first been landed in the Antarctic by the Danish explorer Carsten Borchgrevink in 1899 and most subsequent polar expeditions shared the views of Admiral Richard Byrd who wrote from his camp, Little America, in 1929 that, 'The dogs have delighted me beyond words ... The love that these Eskimo dogs have for their work is quite wonderful ... We can see now that the wisest thing we have done was to insist upon bringing a great many dogs.' However, in late 1991 the Antarctic Treaty nations signed a convention which banned all non-indigenous life forms, except humans, from Antarctica. The huskies would have to go. Even though the dogs have been more or less replaced by motor toboggans and snowmobiles, they are still prized for their hill-climbing ability, good sense on dangerous ice and, most of all, for their companionship. But all dogs must be out of Antarctica by 19 April 1994. As one eminent explorer succinctly reacted: 'The whole thing is a lot of nonsense.'

MAN AND DOG: A WORKING RELATIONSHIP

No one knows how many dogs there are in the world. There are statistics on the dog population of a few countries like the United States, Great Britain and France, but almost all the dogs of Asia, Africa and South America live and die in demographic limbo. A recently published figure claimed that the world dog population was about 400 million, but any estimate must be fanciful and impressionistic. We can say that there are some hundreds of millions of dogs in the world. Some are pampered pets. A far, far greater number are strays or semi-wild and tens of millions are workers – sheep-dogs, cattle-dogs, watch-dogs, sled-dogs.

As the history of dogs in the Antarctic shows, the relationship between man the boss and dog the worker is a difficult one. On the one hand there is sentiment and fine phraseology about 'trusted servants' and 'companions'. On the other hand, expedience and convenience dictate whether a dog will be shot today or tomorrow. Some bargain.

There is, though, a large 'but'. Dogs would not exist in the numbers, variety – or, indeed, for the most part in the comfort – that they do unless they were useful to humans. That usefulness can either be emotional, for example by acting as a pet, or practical – by being a sheep-dog, for instance. For a working dog to be shot at the end of its usefulness may be no more objectionable than for a family pet to be put down for eating one of the grandchildren. The human-dog relationship may be one of great love, devotion, loyalty and heroism, but it is often fundamentally one-sided.

The power that human beings have over dogs has raised a number of moral issues, principally the issue of whether or not dogs themselves have rights. It is something

Pigs are often used to find truffles, the
highly scented fungi that grow in the earth beneath oak trees, but dogs – like the
ones shown in this 1911 advertisement – are less likely to eat the delicacies.

that we will discuss later in 'Dogs and Doctors'. For the moment we can say that what
some people call a worker, other people call a slave.

Because dogs provide a combination of intelligence and strength, obedience and
cunning, they have been more widely employed than any other animal.

Before the development of steam or internal combustion engines – or indeed in
parts of the world where these new inventions were too expensive or too difficult to

The Saint Bernard bringing a flask
of brandy to an avalanche victim is a vivid image of the dog as man's helpmate.
These giants, which can weigh 90 kg (198 lb), were first bred by monks in the Swiss Alps.

maintain – dogs provided cheap, fairly reliable, uncomplaining power. Consider the tiresome work of the turnspit, a small breed that used to run around a circular cage in order to keep a roasting spit turning. Turnspits kept running well into the late nineteenth century.

In places where horses were either unknown or little used, dogs pulled and carried. The Amerindians, like their Inuit cousins, valued them as a source of traction. Among

Even after the arrival of horses,
native Americans continued to use dogs as a means of traction. These Nez Perce Indians,
photographed around 1880, transported their belongings on a dog-hauled travois.

the Indian tribes of the American Great Plains – the Sioux are an example – dogs were used to drag a wooden frame, known as a travois, which could be loaded with food or household goods. When the Sioux eventually acquired horses they were so awestruck by the superiority of their pulling power over that of their previously prized dogs that they called them 'spirit dogs'.

Draught dogs were also in common use in Europe until this century. Breeds like the Leonberger, the Bernese and the Matin Belge hauled produce to market in Switzerland, Belgium and The Netherlands where they provided a cheap alternative

In Europe – especially in the Low
Countries – dogs were a cheap alternative to horsepower even in the twentieth century.
Merchants like this Belgian milkman relied on them to get their goods to customers.

to horses for small farmers and merchants. In 1804 an English tourist in The Netherlands wrote how dogs 'of every description are constrained to promote the trade of the republic with so much rigidity that it is averred that there is not an idle dog in the whole of the seven provinces. You see them in harness at all parts of the Hague, as well as in other towns, tugging at barrows and little carts, with their tongues nearly sweeping the ground and their poor palpitating hearts almost beating through their sides; frequently three, four, five and sometimes six abreast, drawing men and merchandise with the speed of little horses.'

Today sheep-dogs are probably the best known and most numerous of all worker dogs. We have seen that the first dogs were man's companions in the hunt, but when humans exchanged their hunting and gathering way of life for a more pastoral one, dogs were adapted to guard and to help move the herds and flocks. All over the world today they still play an irreplacable role in sheep-farming. In the early 1970s, American sheep-farmers became alarmed because coyotes and other predators were killing more sheep every year. By 1979, the US Government estimated that the total was about 10 per cent of all sheep in the United States. The use of poison, traps and other violent methods to protect flocks was regarded as politically and environmentally unacceptable so two American biologists, Lorna and Raymond Coppinger, were sent to look for other solutions. They soon found an answer to the problem among the sheep-guarding dogs of Europe.

Sheep-dogs fall into two categories: sheep herding and sheep guarding. Herding dogs like collies put on spectacular displays of man-dog co-ordination as they follow the most detailed instructions from the shepherd. Guarding dogs are altogether less

Sheep-dogs can be either
sheep guarding as in this illustration (*above*) or sheep
controlling. The sheep-controlling dog who herds sheep
following the shepherd's command (*right*) is one of the most
beautiful examples of perfect canine-human co-ordination.

The komondor's heavy, corded coat gives
it a very sheeplike appearance and it relies on this camouflage to protect its flock. Predatory
wolves are surprised and frightened when this 'sheep' turns out to be a fierce guard dog.

thrilling to watch in action. They probably developed first among the pastoral people of the central Asian mountains and steppes: remember how the Zoroastrians venerated their sheep-dogs. In such rugged land, flocks live closely with their proprietors and graze in compact groups. They need protecting more than controlling. The sheep-guarding dogs protect them by quite simply *pretending to be sheep*.

In the foothills of the Appenine Mountains in central Italy, shepherds rely on the big breed of dog known either as the Maremma or Abruzzi sheep-dog. These big – up to 40 kilograms (90 pounds) – animals with soft, white coats are both tough and savage. From birth they are raised with the flock. As puppies they play with lambs and are only ever fed on sheep's milk curds or whey. Their job is to blend in with the sheep and protect them from the many wolves that live in the hills. Indeed, they become so protective of 'their' flocks that the shepherd is virtually the only human with whom they can have any relationship. Any stranger, man or beast, is an enemy. Other dogs like the Anatolian shepherd dog from Turkey, the Shar Planinentz from the Balkans and the komondor from Hungary behave in a similar fashion. All these breeds have been brought to the United States to guard flocks, with considerable success.

The Coppingers' experience with sheep-guarding dogs led them to suggest that they were bred to display a particular form of arrested development. As a puppy matures it normally passes through various stages. First, it only wants to stay near its den and may react in a hostile way to the unfamiliar. Then it begins to play with sticks and other objects. The third stage is the development of stalking, when it lies in wait before pouncing. Finally, there is the behaviour known as 'heeling' when the puppy is able to start participating in the hunt with full-grown dogs. The Coppingers believe that sheep-guarding dogs never get further than the first stage. 'They are large volumed, puppy shaped, first stage dogs. They play with each other, but ignore sticks or balls ... They even look like big puppies with their short muzzles and rounded heads, their ears dropped and close to the head,' the Coppingers observe. 'The apparent aggressiveness of [sheep] guarding dogs is derived from that first stage, adverse reaction to novelty and change. It begins with fear-biting and is reinforced as other animals, including humans, react to the panic of a large ... snapping "puppy."' The breeding skills that developed these big 'puppies' have been fiercely guarded for centuries. It was only in the 1930s, for example, that enthusiasts were first able to buy Maremma sheep-dogs for pets.

BREEDING DOGS FOR A PURPOSE

We know that just as man made the dog from the wolf, he also developed particular types or breeds for very specific purposes. Sometimes a dog would be bred to satisfy our aesthetic demands; it might be smaller, or have a silkier coat or a blacker nose, than any other dog. Sometimes, as with the sheep-guarding breeds, the aim would be to develop or reinforce certain 'useful' behaviour.

These functional and aesthetic demands are constantly shifting as time and circumstance move dogs away from the jobs for which they were created. The scrappy little Pembroke Welsh corgi is excellent at herding cattle. It moves the huge beasts

around with ease because it has an extremely well-developed 'heeling' ability: it snaps viciously at the hooves of any recalcitrant cow. As a girl, the then Princess Elizabeth of Great Britain was given a Pembroke by her father. A Welsh cattle-dog may have been an eccentric present for a town-dwelling princess, but the young Elizabeth was soon a devoted corgi owner. Today, that first royal corgi's descendants live in Buckingham Palace and the genetic memory of their ancestral function as herders means the occasional nipped ankle for incautious staff or visitors.

Small terriers (a name derived from the French '*terre*' or earth) have been popular and useful dogs in the Scottish Highlands for at least 500 years. These tough little animals hunted the vermin – foxes, rats and weasels – that tended to set up house in the cairns, or heaps of stone, that were used as burial-markers in Scotland. Cairn terriers were all sorts of colours except white, which was for some reason regarded as undesirable. Any white puppies were drowned at birth.

But sometime early in the nineteenth century, the Malcolm family of Poltalloch in Argyll decided that an all-white terrier would be more easily visible in the rocky landscape. As a result, none of the coloured puppies born to their terriers were used

Eleven Westies – among the first pure white
Scotties bred by the Malcolm family in the late nineteenth century – pose for the camera.

SCOTTIE EPHEMERA

The Scottish or Aberdeen terrier has inspired more design and decoration than any other breed. The black coat, alert expression, extravagant eyebrows and comical silhouette of this wilful and intelligent animal has given birth to socks, clocks and writing paper, pencils and dolls. But the Scottie's most famous appearance is as one half, along with a West Highland

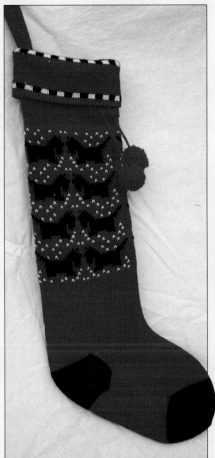

White Terrier, of the duo advertising *Black and White* whisky. In some European countries both breeds are known colloquially as 'whisky dogs'.

The Dobermann pinscher (*above right and right*) was a dog cocktail whose many breed ingredients included Manchester terrier stock (*above left*). The Dobermann's ears are usually cropped in the United States but never in Britain.

for breeding. By the beginning of this century, the Malcolms had produced the pure white dog that we call the West Highland White Terrier, familiar around the world from its use in advertisements for Black and White whisky. Today, virtually all 'Westies' are pets and the dazzlingly white coat, which is emblematic of its once lowly role as a rat-catcher, is now zealously protected as a rather aristocratic badge of breed purity. Like the corgi, the Westie has been upwardly socially mobile and, like the corgi, it still bears the marks of its utilitarian past.

The development of the West Highland White is fairly well documented, but other breeds have more complex histories. An example is the Dobermann pinscher, one of the most celebrated guard-dogs in the world. Unlike most other breeds, which developed gradually and sometimes haphazardly, the Dobermann was the creation of one man, Louis Dobermann. A petty bureaucrat in the German state of Thuringia, he sometimes managed the local dog pound and also worked as a tax collector. His interest in dogs, coupled with the need for a reliable guard to accompany him on his presumably unwelcome rounds, led to the Dobermann pinscher. Dobermann chose to breed a medium-size, intelligent and aggressive dog with a short, neat coat that would not need a lot of looking after. Beginning in about 1865, he mixed together a complex cocktail that included Manchester terrier, Rottweiler, German pinscher, Beauceron and some variety of pointer. Or perhaps he didn't: he kept no records and the breeds used to create the Dobermann pinscher are still hotly disputed by enthusiasts even though it all happened just over a century ago. What is beyond dispute, though, is the dog's success. By 1899, the first official Dobermann shows were organized and the breed's rise to popularity began. Although the period of the First World War was generally not a great time for dog-breeding in Germany – food shortages made the keeping of domestic pets difficult – the Dobermann flourished. This new breed of dog was in demand for use by the German army.

During the Great War all the military powers were busily recruiting and organizing canine corps of messengers, guards and front-line workers. Dogs had fought alongside man since the beginning of organized warfare in the ancient Middle East, but they and their masters had never before been sent to such slaughter. How could man manipulate his best friend's love in a way that could only lead to anguish and 'glorious' death?

CHAPTER SIX

DOGS OF WAR

Early in the fateful summer of 1914, Edwin H. Richardson, a retired British Army officer, was in Russia observing the performance of the Imperial Guards and their dogs on manoeuvre. 'The dogs, when ordered to, left the firing line and pelted away to fetch reserves of ammunition. They returned to their masters with one hundred or more cartridges carried in bags on their backs,' he reported. 'When searching on the battlefield, the Russian dogs have been trained to bring back the caps of the wounded to their keepers ... The dogs also draw miniature Maxims [machine guns] which carry as far as a rifle.' Richardson was clearly impressed by the performance of the Russian dogs, and more convinced than ever that dogs could play a major military role in the coming European war.

Three years later in the midst of the most convulsive and destructive war the world had ever known, he wrote about British army dogs in these, rather human, terms: 'The trained dog considers himself highly honoured by his position as a servant of His Majesty and renders no reluctant service ... Is it not right and just that in the Great War for Principle, when everyone who is brave and good in the Empire, has given of his best, that the dog – man's faithful, loving "pal" – should also be allowed to take part in the great Cause?'

Richardson's work with, and observation of, military dogs was certainly more extensive than that of any man alive. In 1904 ambulance dogs he had trained performed

Dogs have been carefully bred to be aggressive and their controlled aggression has been used in human service since the earliest civilizations. Roman householders hoped to deter burglars with bold mosaics announcing the presence of a fierce dog within.

All the major military powers
made extensive use of dog soldiers during the First World War. Human messengers had
little chance of crossing the hellish no man's land of the Western Front but canine
ones like this German army dog photographed in 1917 did so fearlessly and effectively.

brilliantly with the Russian army during its unsuccessful campaign against the Japanese in Manchuria. Three years later he was supplying guard-dogs to the Ottoman sultan Abdul Hamid in Constantinople, and in the following year Richardson-trained dogs saw action with the Spanish army in Morocco. Richardson travelled through the Balkans and with the Italian army in Libya to observe the effectiveness of sheep-dogs as sentries. In 1911 he sent a sheep-dog and a collie to serve with the Gurkhas on Indian's North-East Frontier.

Richardson was hardly a lone campaigner. Ironically, the growth of scientific warfare with its use of mechanized transport, aircraft, high-velocity long-range artillery and, eventually, armoured vehicles and poison gas created new opportunities for dogs in combat. From about 1900 most of the European powers were developing formal military roles for them. Germany, Russia, Sweden, Italy, France and the Low Countries all had canine soldiers. The military status of the dogs often reflected their civilian roles. In Belgium, for example, where they had been used as draught animals, they were generally employed to pull guns and supplies. In Italy the various common breeds of mountain sheep-dog were trained for use as sentries, particularly with Alpine troops.

Germany was widely regarded as having the most war-ready canine army with about 6000 animals. When the time came to mobilize more dogs the Germans were able to act quickly, aided by a large paramilitary establishment of police dogs and a highly organized national network of dog clubs. Aside from native breeds like Dobermanns, Rottweilers and Weimaraners, they employed dogs from all over Europe. In the years immediately before the outbreak of the Great War German agents had operated in Britain, buying up Airedales and collies. When German troops swept through Belgium and northern France in 1914, promising local dogs were rounded up and sent back to Germany where they were sent to army training camps.

In December 1914 the French newspaper *Le Temps* started a campaign for more French dog soldiers: 'There is no branch of the German war machine that reveals the thoroughness and organization down to the smallest details in preparation for this great war that was expected to place Germany on the pinnacle of success than the method in which the dog power of the country was organized as an auxiliary to the army.' Exact attention to detail even extended to orders for feeding the German war dogs. According to one army order rations were to be 750 grams ($26\frac{1}{2}$ ounces) of dog biscuit and one litre ($1\frac{3}{4}$ pints) of man's warm rations, or 500 grams ($17\frac{1}{2}$ ounces) of meat with either 800 grams (28 ounces) of barley or 1 kilogram (about 2 pounds) of mashed potato. 'Bones,' the order declares, 'are to be given as a special addition.'

In contrast to this methodical Teutonic approach, Britain had only one dog on active service when war broke out: an Airedale serving with the 2nd Battalion, Norfolk Regiment. In spite of the obvious usefulness of dogs to other armies, the British War Office was cool towards Richardson's various proposals. But by 1916 so many army messengers had been killed, and communication between front-line units was becoming so difficult, that Richardson was at last ordered to set up a training school to supply messenger dogs. Patriotic citizens sent their animals to be trained and Richardson dispatched numerous Airedales, lurchers and collies (the preferred breeds) to the Western Front, as well as other, less suitable, dogs like bull terriers, Dalmatians and occasionally an unfortunate King Charles spaniel.

'Would they face the shellfire?' Richardson asked rhetorically. 'Could they be depended on? These questions came to be answered in the affirmative. Yes! They did their duty nobly, passing rapidly through the danger areas and often over land sufficiently impossible of traverse by humans and thus saved countless lives.' Reports from the trenches provide terse and eloquent testimony to the messenger dogs' efficiency: 'The dog dispatched at 12.45 p.m. reached his destination under the hour, bringing in an important message, and this was the first message which we received, all visual communication having failed.' Or, 'On the attack on the Vimy Ridge ... all the telephones were broken and visual signalling was impossible. The dogs were the first to bring through news.'

Following the success of his messengers, Richardson trained other dogs for sentry duty, both in the field and to guard munition dumps and supply depots at home. At the end of the war the canine armies were demobilized. Some were destroyed, many were abandoned and some were adopted by their soldier masters and returned to civilian life. Asking for permission to bring his dog back home, a private in a British infantry regiment wrote: 'He has been a faithful animal to me, both in holding and attacking. I have had him about twelve months, and he was with me all through the retirement of 1918, and with me all through the late attacks since August 1918. He has been slightly wounded twice in going over the top with me ... Kindly do your best for me, as I think he deserves to come home with me, as he has stuck to me through thick and thin, and when I was wounded and could not walk he stayed with me all through the attack under a heavy barrage for nearly three hours, so you can imagine how attached I am to him ...' One war veteran who returned to civilian life became world famous: Rin-Tin-Tin, the first great canine film star. We will discuss him later.

The years leading up to the Second World War once again saw the most aggressive powers – Germany and Japan – methodically building up their canine military establishments, while Britain, France and the United States waited until war had been declared before appealing to civilians to send dogs to take part in the war effort. In the United States, thousands of posters headed 'A Message to America's Dog Owners' went up.

> Total war has made it necessary to call to the colours many of the nation's dogs. Thousands of dogs donated by patriotic men, women and children and trained for special duties with the Armed Forces, are serving on all fronts as well as standing guard against saboteurs at home … New recruits are being inducted daily at the War Dog Training Centers, rushed into training courses which skill them as sentries, message carriers, airplane spotters, pack-carriers – and many other tasks which must remain secret.

The poster went on to call for 'dogs of the larger breeds' including Airedales, boxers, Irish water spaniels and Saint Bernards. While these and many other breeds were drafted into service, Alsatians emerged as the most popular military dogs. Intelligent, strong and trainable, they quickly became more widely recognized for their military prowess than for their historic role as sheep-herders and farmworkers.

Between the wars, Alsatians – originally known as German shepherds, but renamed in a fit of anti-German feeling – had attracted great public attention and sympathy for their use as guide dogs for the blind. The idea was hardly new – a dog can be seen helping a blind beggar on a first-century AD wall-painting found in the ruins of Herculaneum – but it was the start of the modern guide-dog movement with its systematized training methods, a response to the large number of German veterans who had been blinded in the Great War. An American couple who visited the German training school in Potsdam and set up a copy of it in Switzerland in 1928 subsequently popularized guide dogs for the blind.

DOGS IN THE SECOND WORLD WAR

In the Second World War, as in the first, dogs were used to stand guard, to rescue the wounded, to carry ammunition and messages and to lay telephone and telegraph lines. They were also trained to parachute from aeroplanes to accompany raiding or intelligence parties that went deep beyond enemy lines. And, most helpfully to man, and most dangerously for themselves, they were given a new role as mine detectors.

The widespread use of land-mines is one of the most sinister aspects of total warfare that has been developed over the last fifty years. A mine is simply an explosive

DOGS AND STAMPS

Most breeds of dogs have appeared on stamps but the Alsatian
is the undisputed leader of the canine postal pack,
with more representations on stamps than any other breed.

E. H. Richardson, the British father
of modern dog warfare, put these Airedales into training on the eve of the Second
World War. Military dogs looked for wounded soldiers and carried supplies
and messages to endangered outposts in both world wars.

package planted about 30 centimetres (12 inches) underground. When vibrations from, let us say, human footsteps hit the detonator the mine explodes. Some land-mines are big and powerful enough to hurl an automobile through the air. Most tend to be anti-personnel devices that can kill, but more often blow off a foot or a leg. Not only do they cause hideous injuries, they cause them indiscriminately – the victim is as likely to be a woman or child as a soldier. Even worse, a mine, once planted, will wait for years or even decades to explode. Long after hostilities have ceased it carries on the war. The manufacturing and design of small land-mines has 'progressed' to the point where they have become cheap and highly suitable for the 'little' wars that have raged around the world since the 1950s. Modern, non-metallic mines can weigh as little as 50 grams (2 ounces) and can be rapidly sewn over thousands of acres from aeroplanes or helicopters.

Writing in the *New Scientist* magazine in 1991, Eric Stover and Dan Charles pointed out that, 'People in Cambodia and Afghanistan are probably suffering most, but mines also injure large numbers of civilians each year in Mozambique, Burma, Somalia, Ethiopia, Angola, El Salvador and Nicaragua. Even in the Falklands, military units still search for … mines that were scattered from Argentine helicopters across pastures and peat bogs nine years ago.' On a visit to Cambodia – which, thanks to landmines, 'has the highest percentage of disabled inhabitants of any country in the world' – Stover went to a provincial town where 'a group of soldiers scoffed at the idea of clearing the mines they had laid. "Who would be so crazy?" said the oldest. "It would be more dangerous than fighting …" One of his younger companions, a man in his mid-twenties, said: "When we fight, mines are good weapons. But they are bad weapons for farmers and our families." '

Experiments to detect land-mines with infra-red rays, X-rays and radar continue, but dogs remain the best hope for finding these hidden weapons. 'Specially trained dogs, usually Alsatians, are one of the best aids to finding mines,' Stover and Charles write. 'They sniff out the mine's explosive, so they can find a plastic mine that a metal detector misses, and ignore metal objects (such as spent artillery shells) that the detector senses.'

The dog's incredible sense of smell, which helps it to hunt so effectively and to recognize different humans with such accuracy, could prevent the land-mine explosions that ruin life for so many thousands of families each year. Its ability to detect a scent is about one million times more acute than man's – a much greater area of a dog's brain is devoted to the reception and interpretation of smells – and remains well ahead of even high technology.

This ability, combined with keen sight and hearing – the basic equipment that nature gave wolves, assisted by man's selective breeding – has allowed dogs to be as serviceable to man amidst the horrors of the modern battlefield as on the edges of a Stone Age encampment.

DOG WARRIORS OF THE PAST

It is difficult to date the beginnings of organized warfare, but we can say that groups of men were engaged in combat for political ends at about the same time that the first civilizations developed about 6000 years ago. Although there is no evidence that dogs accompanied them, it is hard to believe that they did not. We know that in the sixth century BC the Persian King Cambyses took large packs of dogs with his armies when he invaded Egypt. Xenophon, Pliny and other classical writers record their use in combat and in Rome the memorial column to Marcus Aurelius showed dogs going into battle with the Roman legions. Just as in modern times, dogs would have been tireless and acute sentries. They would also have had an important role in spreading fear and terror among the enemy, a role that Shakespeare uses to metaphorical effect in *Julius Caesar*. When Mark Anthony orders 'Cry "Havoc!" and let slip the dogs of war' in Act Three he is not necessarily making a literal reference to military dogs. It seems quite clear – at least to me – that Shakespeare is hinting that just as a dog can turn savage once human restraint is lessened, so the destructive forces unleashed by war are beyond the control of politicians – even politicians as canny as Mark Anthony. In the prologue to *Henry V* dogs again symbolize the destructiveness of war: 'and at his heels, Leash'd in like hounds, should famine, sword, and fire, Crouch for employment.'

To digress for a moment, many of the references to dogs in Shakespeare's plays are dismissive or derogatory. Perhaps, like most middle-class men of his time, he did not have any particularly fond feelings for them. But in *Two Gentlemen of Verona*, Launce's sarcastic description of his dog's behaviour is so full of affection that I cannot help thinking that Shakespeare must have owned one: 'I think Crab my dog be the sourest-natured dog that lives: my mother weeping, my father wailing, my sister crying, our maid howling, our cat wringing her hands and all our house in a great perplexity; yet did not this cruel-hearted cur shed one tear. He is a stone, a very pebble stone, and has no more pity in him than a dog.'

By Shakespeare's time the use of gunpowder was putting an end to the use of dogs on the battlefield. Although dog armour had been used in combat as protection against arrows and spears, and may be seen in museums or pictured on tapestries, most examples were designed to protect hunting dogs from boar's tusks. For protection against even small arms fire, dogs would have had to be so heavily armoured that they would have been unable to move quickly enough to be of use in battle. So they

Intelligent and powerful, mastiffs
were popular war dogs from ancient times until the Renaissance.
British-born ones were especially prized by the Roman legions.

began to assume their more familiar, to us, role as sentries and, just as important, companions and regimental mascots.

Many of the most famous military commanders insisted on going into combat with their pets. In the eighteenth century the Prussian king, Frederick the Great, was rarely without his pugs and a hundred years earlier the English Royalist general Prince Rupert of the Rhine had been famously distraught when his poodle, Boy, who had accompanied him on so many battlefields, was killed at the battle of Marston Moor in 1644. In 1943, from his post as Supreme Allied Commander during the North African campaign, Dwight Eisenhower wrote to his wife that, 'The friendship of a dog is precious. It becomes even more so when one is so far removed from home as we are in Africa. I have a Scottie. In him I find consolation and diversion ... he is the "one person" to whom I can talk without the conversation coming back to the war.'

Dogs have often been a familiar part of any army on the move. Comforting

Medieval dogs going to war may have been protected by armour like the suits worn by the two animals (*above left*) in a detail from *The Temptation of St Anthony* by Hieronymus Bosch (1450–1516). Dogs also have symbolic military roles as mascots, and breeds like the Irish wolfhound (*above right*) have always been popular.

reminders of civilian domesticity, they are also constant examples of obedience and loyalty – hence their continuing ceremonial role as military mascots. Moustache, a poodle born in Calais in 1799, is typical of many army dogs. Attracted by the noise and motion of a regiment of grenadiers marching through his home town, Moustache abandoned his grocer owner and was adopted by the regimental drum major. One night the dog warned his master of an impending Austrian attack and, 'Next morning it was resolved that Moustache should receive the rations of a grenadier. He was now cropped *a la militaire*, a collar with the name of his regiment was hung around his neck and the barber was ordered to comb and shave him once a week.' Moustache went on to achieve an impressive service record that included a spirited defence of his regimental colours at the battle of Austerlitz even though he had been badly bayoneted. The plucky dog was killed by a cannon-ball at the battle of Badajos, Spain, in March 1811. His grave was marked by a headstone inscribed: *Ce gît le brave Moustache.* (Here

Historically, dogs could be seen on heraldic badges used to show rallying points during battles. The greyhound on Henry VII's emblem (*above left*), in St George's Chapel at Windsor Castle, is an example. More recently, the bulldog personified British pugnacity during the Second World War.

lies the brave Moustache.) There were many other 'Moustaches', and similar stories of dogs fighting spiritedly alongside their masters have always been good for morale. During the Second World War they frequently appeared in newsreels, receiving citations and medals for gallantry.

TOOLS OF OPPRESSION

Inevitably, some episodes in the history of dogs at war are less amusing or inspirational. Dogs have often been used as tools of oppression by totalitarian regimes from the pharaohs to apartheid-era South Africa. Security forces around the world recognize their effectiveness in controlling large crowds. The destructive use of dogs was perhaps never greater than in the Spanish colonization of the Americas.

The historians John and Jeannette Varner believe that Pedro de Vera Mendoza, the Andalusian governor of the Atlantic island of Gran Canaria from 1480, began the practice of using dogs to systematically destroy native populations. He maintained packs of hounds to hunt and kill the indigenous Guanche. When the Spanish conquistadores reached the West Indies they introduced the Mendoza-invented *monteria infernal* or manhunt, a sadistic parody of a stag hunt in which dogs pursued Indians to the death. While such 'sport', warfare and European diseases killed tens of thousands of Indians, others were pressed into service as slave labour in the silver mines of South America. Dogs were used to enforce discipline and pursue anyone who escaped, a practice that was adopted in the slave economy of the southern United States.

Few literary images of dog's cruelty to man are more striking than the pursuit of Eliza, the slave girl, across the ice-covered Ohio River in the pages of Harriet Beecher Stowe's passionately anti-slavery *Uncle Tom's Cabin*. Its status as the best-selling novel of the nineteenth century – shortly after its publication in 1852 it was selling 10 000 copies a week – must have influenced countless readers' feelings about dogs and provided a counterpoint to the growing Victorian sentimentality about them.

In one scene, Eliza's pursuers discuss how best to catch her: ' "I suppose you got

In Harriet Beecher Stowe's
blockbuster anti-slavery novel *Uncle Tom's Cabin* bloodhounds
were the pitiless pursuers of escaped slaves. This demonic image belies
a gentle nature.

good dogs," said Haley. 'First rate," said Marks. "But what's the use? you han't got nothin' o' hers to smell on." "Yes I have," said Haley, triumphantly. "Here's her shawl she left on the bed in her hurry; she left her bonnet, too." "That ar's lucky," said Loker; "fork over." "Though the dogs might damage the gal, if they come on her unawares," said Haley. "That ar's a consideration," said Marks. "Our dogs tore a feller half to pieces, once, down in Mobile, 'fore we get 'em off." ' The diligent and gentle bloodhound, the breed being discussed, has scarcely recovered from this dramatic attack on its character.

Dogs can be, and have been, made to behave cruelly towards humans – we will look at their 'morality' in the next chapter – but, more reprehensibly, humans have used dogs' unconditional love to send them to certain death. During the Second World War, the Russian army trained a number of suicide dogs to attack oncoming German tanks. In training, meat was hidden in tanks to attrack them; in combat, high explosives were strapped to the backs of the dogs who would leap into the tanks, expecting to find food, and be blown up along with the tank crews. The practice was crude, but effective.

In the late 1980s the Israeli army was rumoured to be using similar methods in the Lebanon. In 1989, Animals International reported that, 'Israeli troops used specially trained dogs to carry bombs and gas canisters into guerilla-occupied positions. The dogs were trained to chase enemy soldiers into bunkers and tunnels where the gas was released or the explosives detonated.'

In spite of the dog owner's frequent and affectionate assertions that, 'my dog's not a dog, it's a human' we know that dogs are not humans in dog suits. They have sensory abilities and physical attributes that are far different from ours and, importantly – unlike people – they will, mostly, do what they are told. This obedience can sometimes, as in war, have tragic consequences. But skill, endurance and obedience have also made the dog man's favourite playmate in the pursuit of the unnecessary – sport.

With its keen sense of smell,
the bloodhound is of great helpfulness to man as a finder
of missing persons and extraordinary canine detective.

CHAPTER SEVEN

THE SPORTING DOG

Strip us of clothes, language, politics and religion and you will find a hunting animal. The same hunting animal that millennia ago went 'into business,' as we saw in Chapter Two, with the dog, another hunting animal. That is the basis of the friendship we have been looking at. We know that, for all our human abilities, dogs can do things we cannot. So we bribed, coerced and persuaded them into partnership with us. In his *Meditations on Hunting* the Spanish novelist José Ortega y Gasset reconstructs the moment when man and dogs began to hunt as a team: 'This is the point at which the dog is introduced into hunting, the only effective progress imaginable in the chase, consisting, not in the direct exercise of reason, but rather in man's accepting reason's insufficiency and placing another animal between his reason and the game.' Here we have another good definition of the dog's unique place in the world: an animal who became an intermediary between man and other animals. However, its role was hardly that of a goodwill ambassador. To put it bluntly, people use dogs to kill other animals either for food or for sport. A cursory glance at the names of some breeds is enough to demonstrate just how often we have designed our dogs to hunt or kill. The deerhounds and elkhounds were obviously used to hunt down deer and elk; setters were bred to 'set' or point out game, as were the various pointers; retrievers excelled at returning dead game to their masters; the

Dogs and men are both superbly equipped natural hunters. When hunting changed from being a necessity for survival to a lordly sport the use of dogs in the chase became a subject of great erudition. This fifteenth-century *Traités de Fauconnerie et de Venerie* features a vividly painted boar hunt.

dachshund (*dachs* is German for 'badger') hunted badgers. These breeds and many others are a constant reminder that the dog's most enduring usefulness to man has been in the hunt.

The Hindu myth of how dogs and men came together tells us that when God created dogs he commanded them to serve the most powerful creature on earth. The dog sought out the lion and served him until he found out that elephants were afraid of lions. So he went to serve the lions, until he discovered that lions were afraid of men because men were the greatest hunters on earth. From that moment on dogs helped men to hunt.

I believe there is a profound, spiritual link between dogs and humans that transcends mere convenience. However, my belief is irrational and unprovable and, although it may hurt any dog lover to admit it, dogs – as the Hindu myth shows –

The sixteenth-century Florentine sculptor and goldsmith Benvenuto Cellini captured the appeal of a hunting dog waiting for its master's command.

are amoral and opportunistic. Their obedience is based on food, their 'morality' is entirely that of their master – and, as we have seen time and time again, they give their master unqualified love. To a German shepherd bitch named Blondi, Adolf

Hitler was really quite a nice guy. Man is the only animal with moral sense and our dogs will behave as we have bred and trained them to do, without pondering good and evil.

When dogs kill other animals, or sometimes even each other, as part of human sport, they probably take pleasure in it. I think it is fair to suppose that a dog 'enjoys' his work whether it is rounding up sheep or killing a pheasant. There *must* be some sort of satisfaction when any animal fulfils its genetic destiny. Dogs do not think about whether or not blood sports are cruel – and nor, for the time being, need we.

AN ARISTOCRATIC PASTIME

By the time of the pharaohs, hunting had been transformed from a necessity to the prerogative of the aristocracy. Of course, lowly individuals snared wildfowl and killed vermin, but the hunt was mostly a large-scale, often ritualized, event. You will remember that the highly formal lion hunts of Assyrian royalty symbolized both the king's protective, paternal care for his subjects and his almost superhuman prowess. They involved numerous professional huntsmen and retainers and, of course, numerous dogs. The imagery of the hunt is powerful and full of social and political resonances. For example, the historian David Itzkowitz said of fox-hunting – which we will come to later – that 'Few things seem more English or more aristocratic ... As the almost obligatory hunting prints on the oak or pseudo-oak panelled walls of numerous restaurants, clubs and hotels testify, the power of the sport to evoke images of a particular way of life is very strong.' Some of our most beautiful and profound paintings of dogs have been created as part of the long and full imagery of the hunt.

In the eighteenth century Louis XV of France was famous for his mistresses, his insouciance and his passion for hunting: he spent over 250 days a year in the saddle. He was inevitably a great patron of sporting art, and the greatest of the many painters who worked for him in this field was the academician Jean-Baptiste Oudry. In 1728 Oudry was ordered to follow and record the royal hunts and produced numerous sketches, paintings and tapestries on a heroic scale. The most celebrated is the huge – 180 x 360 centimetre (16 x 12 foot) – oil *Louis XV Hunting the Stag in the Forest of Saint-Germain.* Carefully observed and beautifully painted it is, alas, not a pretty picture. The king and his companions watch from horseback as no fewer than thirty-nine of the royal hounds pursue an exhausted stag to its death in a river. Louis is surrounded

143

MISSE   TVRLU

Jean-Baptiste Oudry (1686–1755)
captured the grandeur and opulence of Louis XV's hunting establishment
in a series of paintings. His huge picture of a royal stag hunt in the
forest of Saint-Germain (*previous page*) shows the most elaborate
form of hunting transformed into a rather gory spectator sport. Oudry also
produced a series of beautifully painted, individually named portraits of
the hunting-mad monarch's favourite dogs (*above*).

by members of his hunting establishment: the Marquis de Beringhen, his first equerry; Prince Charles of Lorraine, the Grand Equerry of France; Monsieur de Fourcy commandant of the hunt; the Marquis de Dampierre, a celebrated composer of music for the hunting horn; and many others.

Oudry's series of royal hunts, which we know by their French name as the *Chasses royales* were more than just a record of a kingly pastime. As an authority on the painter notes: 'The possession of lands and the attendant privilege of hunting were among the most important bases of the legitimacy of monarchy, and their accurate depiction in the *Chasses royales* must be seen as an evocation of more than a thousand years of the history of the Crown of France.' Hunting signified power, hence the severe penalties – sometimes even capital ones – with which poaching was punished. Most of the great European monarchs loved the sport. Charlemagne was an enthusiast, as was another, sixteenth-century, Holy Roman Emperor, Maximilian, whose wife was killed in a hunting accident. As Oudry's painting of the stag's gruesome death shows, these great royal hunts were, in the words of Raymond Carr, 'an upper class ceremony rather than a country sport, a ritualized mass killing, a spectator ceremony rather than a participant sport . . .' The hunts seem to display, and I quote Carr again, 'a delight in the kill' which even contemporary supporters of blood sports find distasteful.

Many of the really great paintings of hunting, particularly those by Dutch artists like Franz Snyders and ones that date from the seventeenth and eighteenth centuries, focus on the kill. And they make much not only of the victim's bewilderment at being brought down, but also of the dogs' almost uncontrollable strength and savagery. I cannot help feeling that this wildness may be over-exaggerated in order to enhance our respect for the man, often a king, who controls them. The dogs become political symbols. Because of their vital role in the royal display, hunting dogs were treated with fantastic care. If we go back to Oudry's big painting of the stag's death, we can read in the catalogue which accompanied its 1750 public exhibition that 'all the horses and all the dogs are exact portraits.'

At Louis XV's command Oudry painted a large number of named portraits of the royal dogs. They are as insightful, and certainly as full of swagger, as those of any – or perhaps I should say any other – court grandee. As we look at them we feel that we are actually getting to know Blanche and Polydore, Misse and Turlu and the other members of the king's kennel. For sheer charm, though, few paintings can outdo

DOGS AS ORNAMENTS

Porcelain and pottery dogs have been made around the world in styles ranging from the refined and aesthetic to the coarse and mass-produced.

RIGHT
This Japanese 'Arita' model of a puppy was made about 1700. It resembles no puppy known to man, but its playful expression and chubby form conjure up images of all puppies everywhere.

The most famous of all dog figurines are the tens of thousands of Staffordshire Dogs produced throughout the nineteenth century. They come in a wide range of colours and sizes but are always distinguished by a haughty stare and magnificently curly ears.

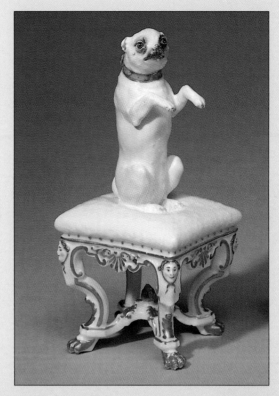

RIGHT *Johann Kandler was the eighteenth century's greatest sculptor of porcelain animals. His Meissen figure of a begging pug, made in 1739, captures the dainty mannerisms of a pampered aristocratic dog.*

LEFT *An eighteenth-century English (probably Coalport) dog, one of a pair copied from Chinese originals made for the European market. Highly stylized, it may represent a British sculptor's interpretation of a Chinese artist's idea of a European dog he had never seen.*

This assortment of British pugs – blunt, somewhat crude and rather stolid – makes an earthy contrast to Kandler's fanciful dog. They are less realistic, but rather more real.

Shooting requires skilled dogs
to locate game, flush it from cover and retrieve it from a distance.
Richard Ansdell's nineteenth-century *Gamekeeper with Dogs* (*left*) provides
a rosy view of a pragmatic working relationship. The harvest-time
scene (*above*) is its twentieth-century equivalent.

Gredinet, Petite Fille and Charlotte, a triple portrait of three of Louis' spaniels. While Petite Fille and Charlotte keenly stalk a red-legged partridge, Gredinet (whose name literally means 'a little knave') chases an emperor moth. It shows a perfect marriage of purpose and playfulness that must enthral all dog owners, regal or otherwise.

The great royal hunts with horse and hound withered and died with the decline of absolute monarchies like Louis XV's Bourbon dynasty. The huge tracts of forests that were required for these stag, deer and boar hunts became increasingly difficult to maintain, as did the armies of retainers and dogs. Shooting replaced hunting on horseback as the royal blood sport – and even the greatest shoots involve fewer, less elaborately organized dogs. In spite of its popularity and the impossibility of shooting without the aid of dogs to flush out and retrieve game, the sport that most people associate with dogs must be another equestrian one: fox-hunting.

THE FOX AND THE HOUNDS

Where some hunting is regal and aristocratic, fox-hunting, as it developed in England and the United States, is a squirearchical or prosperous middle-class pursuit. Its whole history is bound up with that of the dogs that make up the packs.

Fox-hunting developed in England because the traditional royal deer-hunts declined rather more quickly there than elsewhere. The demands of agriculture, in particular, made it harder to maintain the extensive forests they required. Hares were hunted with enthusiasm for some time, but it was the fox that captured the English imagination.

At first fox-hunting was a cumbersome affair. The hunt would assemble at the crack of dawn and a pack of hounds would carefully begin trailing the fox. The earlier the morning start, the slower the fox: foxes feed at night and a full belly meant a sluggish, easy-to-catch prey. When found the fox was usually killed in his hole, underground. The hunting hounds were bred, as Carr describes, 'less for pace than for cry, useful to follow the movements of the pack in a slow teasing woodland hunt.' So it was a leisurely business and perhaps a little boring.

You can see from Carr's description that the dogs worked in a way that might be described as 'assiduous' rather than 'scintillating'; as careful detectives rather than swashbucklers. Then, in the mid-eighteenth century, along came a Leicestershire sportsman and landowner, Hugo Meynell. Like a comet he illuminated and transformed fox-hunting for ever.

Dogs are bred to hunt in a particular fashion and changing their breeding will change the nature of the hunt. Throughout the Middle Ages the best hunting dogs were French. Souillard, a white hound which belonged to Anne de Valois, daughter of Louis XI, was the subject of praise and poetry. In the sixteenth century, Charles IX even wrote his own book about kennel management. However, by the mid-eighteenth century the white hounds of the French royal kennel were being improved by the importation of English stock.

Meynell – it is a joy to say that the name is pronounced to rhyme with 'kennel' – set out to breed faster hounds than before. His idea was that they ought to be able to

Fox-hunting was Victorian England's
most potent image of gentrified country life. All around the world, the iconography
of the hunt was visual shorthand for class, dash and *le style anglais*.

keep up with the foxes as they raced over the grasslands of the English Midlands. As
Carr writes in tribute: 'He was above all a great hound breeder; and the qualities he
sought were those which every great hound breeder has striven to produce, fine noses
and stout running; a combination of strength with beauty and steadiness with high
mettle.' Meynell's success turned fox-hunting into a thrilling, high-speed pursuit. Hunts
started later in the day which, according to David Itzkowitz, brought a whole new
group of people on to the hunting field: the fashionable young who, having stayed up
late into the night gambling and drinking, could not be bothered to get up in time for
a dawn meet.

Meynell began breeding his hounds sometime after 1753 and his innovations spread
rapidly. By the mid-nineteenth century fox-hunting was firmly identified as England's
national sport. The spread of railways at this time made it easy for even town-dwelling
members of the middle class to travel swiftly and easily to good hunting country. The
importance of the dogs coupled with the Victorian obsession with class and breeding,

led to passionate arguments about the ideal hound. When Welsh dogs were introduced for breeding purposes, the hunting enthusiast Lord Bathurst exploded with anger denouncing it as 'a blot on the escutcheon, a *mésalliance.*' His language would not be out of place in a Victorian melodrama about fortune-hunters and heiresses.

Fox-hunting spread to other countries. When the Duke of Wellington embarked on the long and bloody Peninsula Campaign against Napoleon in the early nineteenth century he took his huntsman, Tom Crane, with him. The sight of English officers going from the battlefield to the hunting field with their pack of hounds first bemused and then impressed the Portuguese nobility, who quickly set up their own hunts. Their royal family took to the sport with enthusiasm. King Carlos of Portugal and his son were murdered as they returned from hunting in 1908, presumably too exhausted and exhilarated by the day's sport to be wary of assassins. To this day, many dogs in Portuguese packs still have English names.

Italian fox-hunting has an equally immaculate pedigree. The sixth Earl of Chesterfield devotedly moved to the warm, dry Roman climate when his wife began suffering from consumption. Missing his hunting, he was happy to discover that the broad, grassy expanse of the Campagna, the countryside around Rome, was ideal fox-hunting territory. A hunt was quickly organized and when the earl returned to England in 1837 his friend Prince Odalischi formally founded the Societa della Caccia alla Volpe, the Rome Hunt. For the past 150 years – except during the two world wars – Italians have been treated to the spectacle of pink-coated riders and packs of hounds pursuing foxes through the increasingly built-up Campagna. All the hounds are of English or Irish descent and, even though they are Italian born, are spoken to in English. At their kennels on the Appian Way they are fed on meat and pasta and looked after solicitously by the hunt's almost invariably English or Irish huntsman. The Italian royal family has been closely associated with the Campagna hunt ever since Umberto I became its honorary chairman. The current 'king' of Italy, Umberto II, presides over it from his exile in Portugal.

Like the big royal hunts, fox-hunting requires expensively kept packs of dogs. English foxhounds (*previous page*) were carefully bred from the mid-eighteenth century onwards.

The development of fox hunting followed the same pattern in both Portugal and Italy. It was imported by English aristocrats, expropriated by the local nobility, carried on at high levels of society and conducted with a punctilious regard for English customs. It is different in the United States. A native fox-hunting tradition there dates back to the mid-eighteenth century and demonstrates that while the sport requires support from an élite it is by no means incompatible with democratic principles – as soon as the young George Washington married the rich widow Martha Custis he set up his own pack of hounds. Washington's home state of Virginia remains the *locus classicus* of American fox-hunting.

Although fox-hunting may be relatively informal, at least when compared to the historic royal hunts of Europe, it has the power to evoke ideas about class and tradition derived from its ritual nature, its living link with our ancestral hunting past and the fascination of seeing a large pack of dogs at work. It is a beautiful sport, but for many people a morally troubling one.

For hundreds of years hunting on horseback with packs of dogs was frequently justified by military analogy. What could be better practice for the vital upper-class role of mounted warfare? But hunting, whether for hare, deer or stag, was criticized on moral grounds from at least the twelfth century, as Keith Thomas brilliantly documents in *Man and the Natural World*, and by the late eighteenth century – not long after Meynell's stunning innovations – fox-hunting itself was being attacked on grounds of cruelty.

The novelist Anthony Trollope was among the most enthusiastic and articulate of the sport's Victorian supporters and in the winter of 1869–70 he engaged in a public debate on the virtues of hunting. One of his biographers tells us that, 'Anthony's defence of hunting was not brilliant ... Hunting was a fit pastime for gentlemen, he wrote, because it brought together all classes of society and because it encouraged the virtues of courage and persistence ... it was God's will that animals, and man, should hunt and kill each other.' Writing nearly two hundred years earlier, Edward Bury had imaginatively turned the tables on the hunters by inventing this speech from a dying victim of the hunt: 'Oh man, what have I done to thee ... I am thy fellow creature.'

For our fellow creature, the dog, hunting was no doubt an exhilarating pursuit which guaranteed it a pampered existence. But other sports, more universally reviled, involved considerable cruelty to dogs as part of their 'appeal'. These were bull or bear

Man has often made sport out of cruelty to his best friend. In the name of entertainment dogs have fought against bears, bulls and each other. Thomas Rowlandson (1756–1827) captured the rough and tumble of a crowded dogfight.

baiting, in which bulls or bears were tied to a stake and then attacked by dogs. As the larger animal defended itself the dogs were often bloodied, maimed or killed. The sport was particularly popular in England and Elizabeth I was a keen spectator. A German traveller to Elizabethan London described a 'place built in the form of a theatre which serves for the baiting of bulls and bears. They are fastened behind and then worried by great dogs, but not without risk to the dogs, from the horns of one and the teeth of the other, and it sometimes happens they are killed on the spot. Fresh ones are immediately supplied in the place of those that are wounded or tired.' Another spectator wrote that, 'I believe I have seen a dog tossed by a bull thirty, if not forty, feet high.' Mastiffs were the most common dogs used in these contests, but breeders found that although these big, lumbering animals were incredibly powerful, they were an easy target for a bull. As a result they developed a more compact dog with short, strong jaws and big chest-capacity for endurance in a fierce fight. The result was the British bulldog, which was frequently crossed with terriers to produce the various bull terrier breeds.

Incredibly, bull and bear baiting was not outlawed in Britain until 1835. While the bulldog, which by that time was widely regarded as the country's national symbol, developed into a suprisingly amiable household pet, bull terriers continued to be bred for ferocity and for use in the illicit sport of dog fighting. Charles Dickens, with his usual fine judgement for colourful detail, felt it was just right that Bill Sikes, the homicidal housebreaker in *Oliver Twist*, should have a bull terrier as a pet. Even though Dickens was playing to his readers' prejudices that the breed was thuggish, his sketch of the ailing Bill at home with Bullseye adds considerable warmth to Sikes' otherwise villainous character: 'The dog sat at the bedside: now eyeing his master with a wistful look, and now pricking his ears, and uttering a low growl as some noise in the street, or in the lower part of the house, attracted his attention.'

Today other breeds have become popular for use in fights. It is, I think, much to our human shame that even though dog fighting mostly exists today in covert form, it is widespread and popular. One of the few places where it is carried on more or less in the open, with a large degree of ceremony and a relatively small amount of savagery, is in the Kochi prefecture of the island of Shikoku in south-western Japan – the home of the Tosa fighting dog.

THE TOSA FIGHTING DOG

Tosas were traditionally the fighting dogs of the samurai warrior caste and Tosa fighting was reputedly encouraged as a vicarious form of combat. It was hoped that rather than feuding with each other the samurai would sublimate their aggression through their dogs. Towards the end of the Tokugawa shogunate in the mid-nineteenth century, when Japan was opened up to Europeans, a bulldog owned by a British missionary was mated with some native Tosa bitches. The mixed-breed offspring were the forerunners of the modern Tosas and were further crossbred with other foreign dogs, including mastiffs and pointers, to produce a bigger and more aggressive breed.

Even as the samurai's power was being eroded by the reforms of the late nineteenth-century Emperor Meiji, Tosa fighting was becoming more popular and more formalized. By the early stages of the Second World War the Tosa was playing for the Japanese the sort of symbolic role its ancestor the bulldog played for the British. It was seen as an embodiment of the national will to win and Tosas even toured the front lines to boost the morale of Japanese soldiers. But their national glory was short-lived. As the military tide turned and food shortages began to afflict the civilian population, Tosas with their huge appetites began to be regarded as unpatriotic. All the dogs in Kochi were destroyed. However, ten that had been evacuated to the north of Japan survived and became the parents of the post-war generation of dogs.

Tosas were losing their social status, though, and increasingly becoming the favoured pets of the Yakuza, the widely recognized gangs that reputedly control organized crime in Japan. They are thought to bring a chivalric gloss to the Yakuza's often mundane activities and, just as with the samurai, their fights are felt to provide a form of ritual combat between rival groups. These formidable dogs – a Tosa can tip the scales at 80 kilograms (176 pounds) – are dressed in elaborate costumes for their pre-fight parades and face each other in a ring. The contest is conducted according to strict rules. In keeping with the occasional Japanese taste for silent self-mortification when matters of honour are involved, Tosas are disqualified if they bark or cry during even the most painful moments of combat.

Supporters of Tosa fighting will maintain that it is not cruel, that the dogs love

In Japan, Tosa fighting dogs (*left*) are elaborately dressed and paraded before going into the ring to take part in highly ritualized combat. Food shortages almost killed off the breed during the Second World War.

Greyhounds (*right*) may be the oldest breed of dog still in existence. Once the favoured pets of royalty, they are now popular proletarian entertainers on the race track. These dogs are running on Australia's Gold Coast.

to fight, that the animals would hardly exist if there were no such organized contests, and so on. But one man's sport is another man's cruelty. Richard Martin, nicknamed 'Humanity Dick', was a vocal nineteenth-century opponent of bull baiting and campaigner for better treatment of cab horses. He was also a keen scourge of the fox and hunted over his own 2000-acre estate in Ireland.

It is clear that the sporting use of dogs will inevitably involve aggression, either towards other dogs or other animals – even if that other 'animal' is only the tin rabbit that greyhounds chase around a track to the delight of onlookers and bookmakers. At war, at work or in the field, we have looked at how the controlled aggression of dogs has been used in the service of man. But what happens when dogs bite the hands that feed them?

CHAPTER EIGHT

DOGS AND DOCTORS

After being bitten by a rabid dog, the victim might begin to experience some symptoms within a couple of weeks. But the rabies virus can lie hidden like a land-mine and it may be some months before the disease begins to manifest itself. The original bite may be long healed, but numbness or tingling around the spot will hint that something is not quite as it should be. The victim may start to experience volatile changes of mood, either talking rapidly or falling into periods of sullen silence. There may be headaches, loss of appetite and difficulty in sleeping. By now the tiny, bullet-shaped rabies virus is spreading through the nervous system.

As the brain becomes increasingly affected, the victim begins to show the fear of water that has so impressed and terrified observers for thousands of years. He wants to drink, but can't because the sight of water causes such violent terror that there are horrible spasms of the diaphragm: spasms so intense that the connection between the oesophagus and the stomach can be ripped in two. The sight, the sound and sometimes the thought of water is torture. Stimuli like bright lights and loud noises can also bring on paroxysms of choking. At this stage, the vocal chords become so swollen that when the victim screams in pain or fear he begins to sound like a dog barking. The victim is now in a state of such mental agitation that he may become violent and paranoid.

Rabies turned our best friends
into objects of fear and terror. This woodcut, from a 1566 edition
of the work of the Greek physician Dioscorides (c.40–c.90 AD),
shows two men trying to kill a rabid dog.

The choking fits become more and more crippling. The victim either chokes to death or dies of exhaustion. All this happens within about three to five days of the first symptoms showing themselves.

A dog suffering from rabies will go through similar miserable stages. For two or three days, in the prodromal stage of the disease, it will behave abnormally. A friendly animal will become withdrawn and growl suspiciously; an aggressive one will suddenly become affectionate. Then, as the disease develops and moves into the excitative stage, the dog will become irritable, restless and snappy. The tone of its bark will change and paralysis of the pharynx will make it drool saliva – hence the popular image of the rabid dog 'foaming' at the mouth. Finally, there will be convulsive seizures, overall paralysis and death.

The name rabies derives from the Sanskrit *rabhar*, 'to do violence'. The disease is also sometimes known as hydrophobia from the Greek for 'fear of water', its most remarkable symptom. The Greeks themselves simply called it *lyssa* – 'madness'. Rabies affects all warm-blooded animals; it can be transmitted by bats or foxes, badgers and even mongooses, but humans generally get it from dogs. It is the single greatest irony of the human-dog relationship that this most terrible, fatal and fearsome disease should come to us from our best friend. In contrast to all the bonds of love, empathy, convenience and utility that tie man and dog together, rabies is the chasm that separates the two. It seems like an act of betrayal, a sign not just of a dog gone mad, but a whole world gone mad.

The disease has been well known and feared for over 4000 years. It is cited in a Babylonian law code of *c.* 2300 BC: 'If a dog is mad and the authorities have brought that fact to the knowledge of its owner; if he does not keep it in, it bites a man and causes his death then the owner shall pay forty shekels of silver.' Rabies has been carefully observed ever since. 'The idea of rabies being a contagious disease transmitted by biting animals was certainly familiar to Aristotle and was mentioned by Hippocrates in the fourth and fifth centuries BC,' the zoologist David Macdonald tells us. 'Interestingly, Aristotle maintained that while mad dogs infected other animals with their bites, they did not apparently infect man; another surprising aspect of ancient writings is that ninth-century Byzantine authors thought rabies to be a curable disease.'

We have seen that much of the hatred displayed towards dogs by some Middle Eastern religions was caused by the large number of strays in the region – strays that

Rabies periodically swept through the Middle East.
The horror is elegantly represented by a Persian miniature-painter of the Baghdad school (*above*).

The ancient Greeks began the study
of veterinary science. The care of valuable animals like royal hunting dogs was much
discussed and written about. 'Caring for the Hounds' from Gaston Phebus's fifteenth-century
Le Livre de la Chasse (*overleaf*) shows a range of rudimentary canine first aid.

165

could periodically become infected with rabies. It is an epidemic disease that comes in waves and there may well be some correlation between outbreaks in the Middle East and the amount of religious agitation against dogs. Its current high incidence in continental Europe is part of an epizootic – an outbreak of a disease among animals – that can be accurately dated and placed as having started just south of Gdansk, Poland in 1939.

Diseased animals can spread rabies swiftly. Macdonald tells us that on one day in 1851 a rabid wolf attacked and bit forty-six people. The equation is terrifying: one day, one animal, forty-six deaths. Understandably, attempts to control the disease were often brutal. When rabies broke out in central London in 1752 *all* dogs were ordered to be shot. Attempts at treating bites ranged from the inept – cauterizing the wound with burning iron – to the superstitious – a visit to the shrine of St Hubert near Liège. All were hopeless.

Geographically widespread, invariably fatal and agonizingly spread by an animal we love and trust, rabies was among man's greatest fears. Its cure was one of the inspirational success stories of the history of science

PASTEUR AND THE CURE FOR RABIES

In the nineteenth century a number of chemists and doctors began to agree with the idea that most human diseases were spread by tiny organisms or microbes. The German physician Robert Koch and the French chemist Louis Pasteur were two of the most tireless workers in the search to discover and explain the mechanism of disease. Koch discovered the microbes that were responsible for tuberculosis and cholera. Pasteur conquered diseases in wine and beer, sheep, cattle and silkworms before he became one of humanity's great saviours with his work on rabies.

Before the nineteenth century scientific understanding of the disease was minimal. Then there were two breakthroughs. The first was the realization that it is carried by the saliva of the infected animal. The second, that it is essentially a disease of the nervous system.

As a small child growing up in the remote and mountainous Jura region of France, Pasteur had firsthand experience of rabies. A young girl in his village was bitten by a rabid wolf; her wound was treated with a red-hot iron poker at the neighbourhood smithy; the girl went mad and died. France had been afflicted with rabies ever since the first reported outbreak there in AD *c.* 900 but people were particularly aware of it during the nineteenth century.

In many ways rabies occupied much the same position during Pasteur's lifetime as AIDS in the 1980s and 1990s. Other causes of death were more statistically significant: in *The Animal Estate* Harriet Ritvo tells us that, for example, 'the average English citizen of the late nineteenth century was more than ten times as likely to be murdered as to die of hydrophobia.' But the method of transmission of rabies and its horrible symptoms made the search for a cure a particularly emotive issue.

Pasteur was nearly sixty and already famous when he began his experiments with rabies in 1881. He started by injecting saliva from a rabid child into a rabbit. The rabbit developed the disease, but in a series of subsequent experiments Pasteur failed

The scientist as hero: Louis Pasteur
(1822–95) in his glory, microscope at the ready. Conqueror of diseases
of wine, beer and silkworms, reviled by some as a 'physiological terrorist',
Pasteur's vaccine against rabies won him the civilized world's gratitude.

to isolate the offending microbe. Eventually, one of Pasteur's assistants, Emile Roux, suggested that they must work directly with living nerve tissue. He went on to suggest that rabies should be introduced to a dog's nervous system by trepanning – boring a shaft through its skull. Pasteur objected at first but then agreed. The dog recovered quickly from the operation. Roux describes his master's inspection of the animal: 'Pasteur did not love dogs; but when he saw this one full of life, curiously ferreting about everywhere, he showed the greatest satisfaction and straightaway lavished upon him the kindest words. He felt an infinite liking for this dog which had endured trepanning without complaint and had thus relieved him of scruples concerning the operation.'

If Pasteur had scruples about the operation, he had none about its result. As hoped the animal contracted rabies within a fortnight and the laboratory performed the operation on numerous other dogs. René Dubos, Pasteur's biographer, explains its significance: 'Thus was discovered a technique for the cultivation of an unknown infectious agent in the receptive tissues of a susceptible animal. This technique has permitted the study of those agents of disease which are not cultivable in lifeless media, and has brought them within the fold of the germ theory of disease.'

Through his work on chicken cholera, Pasteur had discovered that it was possible to 'attenuate' or weaken disease-causing microbes and use them to manufacture vaccines in the laboratory. The vaccination technique – whereby a weak strain of a disease is injected into the body to build up its immune system so that it can fight off a full-blown attack of the same disease – had been discovered nearly a century before by the English physician Edward Jenner, who had vaccinated patients with cowpox as a preventative against its more virulent cousin smallpox. Pasteur's discovery that vaccines could be manufactured meant, in Dubos' words, that, 'instead of depending upon the chance finding of naturally occurring immunizing agents, as cowpox for smallpox, vaccination could then become a general technique applicable to all infectious diseases.'

Once it had become possible for Pasteur to create rabies on demand by using laboratory animals, including dogs, it was almost inevitable that he would be able to develop a successful vaccine. Because rabies develops relatively slowly, he was convinced that vaccination after the bite would prevent the disease from pursuing its fatal course. Experiments with dogs gave encouraging results.

By March 1885 Pasteur was anxiously waiting to use the newly developed technique. 'I have not yet dared to treat humans,' he wrote, 'after bites from rabid dogs; but the time is not far off, and I am much inclined to begin on myself – innoculating myself with rabies and then arresting the consequences for I am beginning to feel very sure of my results.' Nevertheless, he was not yet prepared to inject a human with even a weak version of rabies. Four months later, he was forced to act. A nine-year-old boy from Alsace, Joseph Meister, was attacked by a rabid dog and bitten fourteen times. Two and half days later he arrived in Paris to see Pasteur. 'The death of this boy seemed inevitable and I decided not without lively and cruel doubts, as one can believe, to try in Joseph Meister the method which had been so successful in dogs.' Meister recovered and later became the proud gate-keeper of the newly created Pasteur Institute. Fifty-five years later, in a cruel footnote, this first survivor of the rabies vaccine committed suicide rather than allow invading German soldiers to enter into Pasteur's crypt.

Within sixteen months of the first treatment, 2490 people had been successfully vaccinated by the Pasteur method. Within fifty years, a total of 51 107 patients had been treated at the Institute with only 151 deaths. Rabies remains a scourge, especially in the Third World, but the hopeless terror it inspires has all but gone. Pasteur became a universal hero, showered with praise and honours. But his breakthrough was psychological as well as medical. He freed mankind to love dogs without fear.

ANIMAL EXPERIMENTATION

There is, however, the vexed question of vivisection – the use of living animals for scientific experiments. The practice was becoming controversial even during Pasteur's lifetime and still haunts us today. As his assistant Roux tells us, Pasteur did not like vivisection, but still used living animals when he thought it necessary to do so.

When Pasteur was just beginning his work on rabies he, along with Robert Koch and over 3000 eminent scientists and doctors, took part in an International Medical Congress in London in the summer of 1881. The vivisection debate was in the air and the delegates addressed the issue. They passed a resolution: 'That this Congress records its conviction that experiments on living animals have proved of the utmost service to medicine in the past, and are indispensable to its future progress; that, accordingly, while strongly deprecating the infliction of unnecessary pain, it is our opinion, alike in the interests of man and of animals, that it is not desirable to restrict competent persons in the performance of such experiments.' To Pasteur and many of his colleagues the issue was relatively simple. If man could benefit from the use of animals in the laboratory, and if that use was not gratuitously cruel, then animals must be sacrificed for the health and happiness of man. This was, after all a greater moral good than the health and happiness of animals. Opponents of animal experimentation described the pro-vivisectionsists as 'physiological terrorists'.

Vivisection is almost as old as medicine itself. To researchers like the Roman physician and vivisectionist Galen, man as the only living creature endowed with a rational soul could use animals as he liked for his convenience and enlightenment. Biblical authority – 'Let him have dominion over the fishes of the sea, and the birds of the air, and the beasts of the earth' – also reinforced man's command of the animal kingdom. For centuries science and medicine were firmly anthropocentric. Realdo Columbo, the sixteenth-century anatomist who performed horrific experiments with living animals, including the dissection of a pregnant bitch in front of an audience of clergymen, also praised 'the happy dog because he affords to us a sight for acquiring knowledge of the most beautiful things.' Columbo made important and interesting discoveries such as the way in which blood circulates around the lungs, but there was a growing unease that animal experimentation, no matter how useful and no matter how beneficial to man, was somehow wrong.

Two centuries after Columbo's experiments, the German philosopher Immanuel Kant expressed his belief that cruelty to animals could coarsen man: 'If a man shoots his dog because the animal is no longer capable of service, he does not fail in his duty to the dog, for the dog cannot judge, but his act is inhuman and damages in himself that humanity which it is his duty to show towards mankind … he who is cruel to animals becomes hard also in his dealing with men.' But Kant did believe that animals were a means to an end, and that 'That end is man'. His contemporary, the English philosopher Jeremy Bentham, considerably raised the moral stakes when he formulated the argument we have already discussed in connection with fox-hunting: 'The question is not, Can they reason? nor, Can they talk? but, Can they suffer?' After Bentham more and more people began to feel that animals had to be considered, not in terms of their utility to man but in terms of their own fundamental rights to a life as free from suffering as possible.

Dogs are intelligent but obedient subjects for human research. Leonardo da Vinci carefully and inquiringly drew them (*below left*); the Russian physiologist Ivan Pavlov (*above*) observed their reactions to particular stimuli as part of his research into conditioned reflexes; and Russia's Laika was the first living creature in space.

Dog lovers and others have been shocked by photographs of experiments such as the one in which beagles were forced to chain-smoke thousands of cigarettes – the most widely publicized of all 'medical' tortures inflicted on dogs in the name of research. But, such sensationalism aside, do we believe that our human rights to health and happiness are greater than those of our fellow creatures? Do we feel that a flea or a mouse or a chicken can be made to suffer, but not a dog or a dolphin or a chimpanzee? Understanding the justifications of scientific research is one of the greatest difficulties that ordinary people face. Do scientists really need to use dogs and other animals?

George Bernard Shaw brilliantly satirized the issue in his 1932 story 'The Black Girl in Search of God'. When the girl screams in terror at the sound of a lion's roar, an old man explains that she was merely performing a conditioned reflex. 'This remarkable discovery,' the old man elaborates, 'cost me twenty-five years of devoted research, during which I cut out the brains of innumerable dogs, and observed their spittle by making holes in their cheeks for them to salivate through instead of their tongues. The whole scientific world is prostrate at my feet in admiration of this colossal achievement and gratitude for the light it has shed on the great problems of human conduct.'

'Why didn't you ask me?' the girl replied. 'I could have told you in twenty-five seconds without hurting those poor dogs.'

What could science tell us 'without hurting those poor dogs'? If scientists say that a certain amount of animal suffering, sensibly limited, is necessary to alleviate the distress and ill health of thousands of human beings, do we agree? Some people have clear-cut and fervently believed answers, positive or negative, to these questions. I – and I suspect I am like most people on this issue – just don't know. In a counterblast to the views of the animal rights movement, the English academic Peter Carruthers writes that he finds it 'intuitively abhorrent that the lives or sufferings of animals should be weighed against the lives or sufferings of human beings.' He goes on to

Beagles may have descended from
ancient Greek hunting dogs. Compact, resilient and keen to please
they have sadly attracted the attentions of medical researchers.
Images of beagles in laboratories stunned animal lovers.

TOY DOGS

Toy, miniature and other very small dogs have sat on ladies' laps, slept in mandarins' sleeves, and endlessly enthralled as tiny companions physically far removed from their wolf ancestors.

RIGHT *In* Dynamism of a Dog on a Leash (1912) *the Italian futurist Giacomo Balla neatly captures the nervous energy of a long- haired miniature dachshund out for a stroll with its mistress.*

ABOVE *This painting of a terrier by an unknown artist in c.1860 encapsulates all the appeal of an ever-popular breed.*

Abraham van den Tempel's Two Dogs in a Park *places a pair of spaniels in a picture and creates an image as full of power, money and breeding as it would be if their aristocratic master had been included.*

A small dog sleeps on its owners' bed in this sixteenth-century, German stained-glass panel.

ABOVE *This mischievous little dog lends a touch of playful domesticity, and perhaps even more symbolism, to van Eyck's allegory-laden* The Arnolfini Marriage.

The long-haired Chihuahua, first bred in Mexico, was a popular ladies' dog in the 1920s.

LEFT *The Lowchen – now one of the rarest breeds in the world – enjoyed its heyday as one of the favoured lap-dogs of eighteenth-century European aristocrats. This is reputed to be a portrait of one that belonged to Louis XV's mistress, Madame de Pompadour.*

maintain that 'there are no good moral grounds for forbidding hunting, factory farming or laboratory testing on animals.' For Carruthers, as for Kant and many others, animals are there to be used. Before dog owners are stirred with indignation, I must point out that many people who live most intimately with their dogs – the Arctic explorers are an example – also treat them pragmatically.

As my last word on the subject, I would commend some pragmatic thoughts from the philosopher and physiologist Bernard Rollins, who writes, 'There are a great many physical disanalogies between humans and animals, many of them quite glaring … the physical disanalogies seem to be far more glaring than many of the mental ones. I am no less comfortable with the conclusion that what seemed to control a rat's pain will control mine than with the conclusion that what caused a rat's tumour will cause one in me.' The debate is unlikely to be resolved in our lifetimes.

'COMPANION DOGS'

Dogs thankfully have a medical and scientific role away from the possible horrors of the research laboratory. The success of guide dogs for the blind encouraged the training of dogs for a variety of 'companion' uses that are both practical and therapeutic. They can be trained, for example, as 'service dogs' to help the wheelchair bound, or to act as a pair of ears for the profoundly deaf. In the United States, service dogs have been trained in an innovative programme which has benefited both recipients and trainers. In 1980, a former inmate of a women's prison conceived a dog-training programme for prisoners which she hoped would help them feel they were 'contributing something worthwhile to society'. Two years later the inmates of the euphemistically named Purdy Treatment Center for Women – a maximum security prison in Washington state – began their work in the Prison Pet Partnership programme. The women, who were all serving long sentences for crimes ranging from serious fraud right up to murder, were given an intensive course in dog care and training. Some of the dogs, the so-called 'Paroled Pets', were rescued from the local pound and were groomed, obedience-trained and made fit for new lives as family pets. Others, also rescued, were trained to be service dogs for the handicapped. 'Inmates make a positive contribution to the community,' the organizers claim. 'People receive well-trained dogs, and dogs which would have been destroyed as unwanted animals find loving homes.' The programme has been successful enough to be adopted elsewhere. 'It's made this time bearable,' a prisoner said, 'and something for me to look forward to every day. Most important, it keeps channels open to the outside world. It's so easy to get caught up in the life here and lose touch with the free world.'

Some of the dogs trained by the women prisoners have been used therapeutically. For reasons which we cannot understand, severely disabled people sometimes respond to the attentions of a dog even when nothing else has roused them. At the prison in Washington a seven-year-old girl girl, severely disabled by cerebral palsy, responded positively to the licks and nuzzles of a mongrel. Perhaps the ancients were right when they praised the healing power of a dog's lick. It is now widely accepted that dogs can play a useful part in lowering blood pressure, curbing mental agitation and soothing anxious or lonely patients.

In Britain dogs are frequently used for hospital therapy, particularly with elderly patients. In one study an attempt was made to assess the therapeutic effectiveness of a dog's visit to two psychiatric wards, one housing twenty-seven sufferers from senile dementia and the other home to twenty-one depressed elderly patients. The wards were observed for a month. 'Direct observation records suggest that the patient's behaviour improved markedly in the dog's presence,' the *Nursing Times* reported. 'The nurses rated the visits made [by a therapeutic dog] very positively. Generally nurses in both wards said they made the patients "better than usual."' The study suggested that patients interacted with each other much more frequently when a dog was present, and that they spoke more and with greater coherence. 'We are cautiously optimistic about the value of companion pets,' the report continued. 'Given the practical benefits, we suggest that nurses consider using companion pets with their patients.'

The dogs of science may once again be healers and nursemaids, rather than 'experimental aids' to be imprisoned and slaughtered in the name of research.

Labradors are popular 'companion dogs'.

CHAPTER NINE

STARRING DOGS

A 1932 newsreel proclaimed the news to grief-stricken audiences: 'Rin-Tin-Tin plays his final role ... wonder dog of the movies is dead after being idol of audiences both young and old.' The sixteen-year-old German shepherd died with a tearful Jean Harlow at his bedside. 'Rinty' had been voted the most popular film star in the United States for two years running and probably earned more money for the fledgling Warner Brothers film studios than any of their human stars.

Like many other all-American heroes, Rinty was an immigrant. Just before the end of the First World War, Leland Duncan, an American sergeant, found a German shepherd and her litter of five puppies in a ruined airfield in France. Duncan took one of the puppies back home to California and Rinty grew up to be a film star. His first film, *Where the North Begins*, was a minor hit, but when the young Darryl F. Zanuck, who went on to be one of Hollywood's most powerful moguls as founder of Twentieth Century Fox, began writing his scripts, Rinty swiftly became the best-loved dog in America. His first Zanuck-inspired film, *Find Your Man* (1924), led to a succession of smash hits. His ex-army owner earned a $5 million fortune from his particular share of the spoils of war. 'Rin-Tin-Tin could do anything,' Zanuck reminisced to his biographer Mel Gussow. He also claimed that as many as 'five or six' Rin-Tin-Tins were used in each film.

Unlike human actors, most of whom were unable to make the traumatic change in acting technique from silent films to sound, the non-speaking Rinty's talent flourished in the new medium, and audiences were thrilled to be able to hear his, I must say rather less than sonorous, bark for the first time. When he died at the advanced age

America was the land of opportunity
for the German Rin-Tin-Tin, as it was for many other immigrants. Here the
most popular film star of his time has a final grooming from owner
Lee Duncan before starting work on *Jaws of Steel*.

Elizabeth Taylor starred opposite Lassie in two feature films. This happy scene is from the 1944 tear-jerker *The Courage of Lassie*. But did Taylor know that Lassie was a laddie? The male collie was the greatest female impersonator in screen history.

of sixteen, the nation's grief was short-lived. He was replaced by his son Rinty II, who carried on in the family business until eclipsed by a greater star: Lassie.

As the centre of attention in the tearful blockbuster *Lassie Come Home*, the collie easily stole the limelight from her co-stars Elsa Lanchester, Roddy McDowall and Elizabeth Taylor, who was also in her first starring role. Metro-Goldwyn-Mayer, delighted with the success of their own dog star, commissioned a succession of further films and in the years immediately after the Second World War Lassie starred in a series of seven respectably profitable movies. Her film star looks belied her breed's history as tough, Scottish herding dogs, officially known as rough coated collies. Some time early in the nineteenth century they were crossed with Russian wolfhounds to produce the glamorously attenuated, silky coated dogs we are familiar with today. Queen Victoria, that tireless font of canine fashion, introduced collies into society when she brought some back to England after a Scottish holiday at Balmoral in 1860.

The secret of Lassie's success was her magnificent coat and eyes that rivalled even those of Bette Davis for luminosity and expressiveness. Her hidden shame was that 'she' was a male. The original Lassie had problems with her coat just before the start of filming for *Lassie Come Home* and her stand-in, a male called 'Pal', was called upon to assume the starring role. Pal became Lassie, the most famous dog and – I suppose – transsexual in film history. Just as Rin-Tin-Tin was succeeded by his son, 'Pal' sired a succession of Lassies. The seventh generation is at work in Hollywood today under the tutelage of Bob Weatherwax, son of Rudd Weatherwax the trainer and owner of the originals.

The dynastic nature of canine stars explains some of their appeal to film companies. Despite the dog's short life span, they can appear to live for ever as they are seamlessly replaced by look-alikes. Unlike their human counterparts, even the most celebrated dogs don't command huge fees for performing. So even though making dog films – which after all rely on complicated stunts rather than acting – can be technically demanding, the economics are attractive. Dogs can be relatively cheap, relatively reliable and certainly enduring stars. None the less, although the appeal of Rin-Tin-Tin and Lassie reached mythic status, that of subsequent dog stars of film and television – including Benji, Tequila and the long-forgotten Strongheart, star of the first dog hit *The Silent Call* in 1921 – has been less long lasting.

The search for canine stars is unceasing – a suburban Saint Bernard named Beethoven is the latest aspirant – but when a real dog won't do one can be invented with animation. Surprisingly, dogs were only supporting characters in the great classics of 1920s and 1930s animation. Walt Disney's Goofy and Pluto had their devotees, but dogs were consistently overshadowed by a growing menagerie of talking rabbits, mice and even a woodpecker. None the less, two of Disney's full-length cartoons featuring dogs – *The Lady and the Tramp* (1956) and *One Hundred and One Dalmatians* (1961) – are among the most popular animated films ever. When Disney decided to film Dodie Smith's novel about Dalmatians he changed the history of an already notable breed. His research was assiduous. Before work started on the film he sent a film crew to

183

After the huge success of Walt Disney's
1961 cartoon *One Hundred and One Dalmatians* (*above*), sales of the one-time carriage dog
shot up. Active and dazzlingly showy in their spotted coats, Dalmatians were
familiar sights in small-town America where they worked as fire station mascots (*right*).

France to document the behaviour of a family of Dalmatians owned by the Comtesse
de Quelen, an aristocratic and highly regarded fancier of the breed. Soon after the
film opened, the price of Dalmatian puppies tripled as children begged their parents
for one of their own.

It was not as if the breed had been obscure before it got the Disney treatment.
The Dalmatian's extraordinarily showy, black-spotted coat has always made it widely
recognized. Bred with incredible endurance and a love of long-distance running, it
has been associated with horses for centuries. In 1847 William Youatt wrote that the
Dalmatian was 'clearly distinguished by his fondness for horses and as being a frequent
attendant on the carriages of the wealthy. To that office it seems to be confined, for it
rarely develops sufficient sense or sagacity to be useful in any of the ordinary offices
of the dog.' Horse-drawn fire engines remained in use in the United States into the

first decades of this century, and as the private use of carriages declined Dalmatians found a new 'office' as the fireman's companion. Even when fire brigades abandoned horses, the dogs remained behind as fire station mascots.

Because the breed was not only distinctive and easily recognizable, but also associated with the altruism and bravery of firemen, Dalmatians were inevitably attractive to salesmen and advertisers. They were used to promote a number of products, some ephemeral – like Fatima cigarettes, whose 1927 packet featured a Dalmatian wearing a green collar – and others more enduring, like Texaco petroleum whose trade mark of a T and a star adorned the fire helmet worn by Sparky the Texaco Dalmatian for many years.

DOGS AS SALESMEN

The development of the mass media – high speed printing, photographic reproduction, moving pictures and ultimately television – went hand in hand with the growth of our modern commercial society. Products manufactured on a huge scale could be sold to a large number of people through words and images efficiently produced and disseminated through the new means of communication. Generic products became specific brands, people became consumers – and dogs became salesmen. It was quickly realized that they are rich in what we now call 'associational values'. They immediately conjure up images of home and family, love and loyalty – images that can be used to sell products. When the British company ICI launched the television advertising campaign for its Dulux paint in 1961 they chose an Old English sheep-dog as their symbol. They felt that this classless, warm and slightly comical animal would make buyers feel some sort of affection for what an advertising executive described as 'a tin of cold white chemicals'. Dulux became the leading brand of British paint. But the advertising campaign did not just sell paint. It inadvertently sold sheep-dogs too, and the rather hard-to-control breed became a British family favourite.

The most celebrated of all selling dogs, though, was one of the first: Nipper, a

W hat does an Old English sheep-dog have to do with a tin of paint? Not a lot really, other than its ability to be such an effective salesman of so unemotional a product that it is often referred to as the Dulux dog.

English Rose

SALESDOGS

Dogs sell because we trust them: their associational values conjure up feelings of family, fidelity and truthfulness. They have remained one of the most powerful images in the arsenal of commercial persuasion.

A mournful-looking basset hound could sell anything with those big eyes and long, droopy ears. In this case, the dog is peddling a brand of suede shoes and connected to the product by a subliminal pun: in the United States 'dogs' are slang for feet.

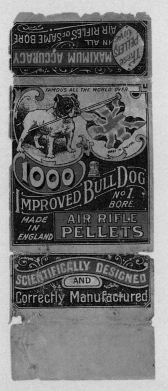

Bull Dog air-rifle pellets shamelessly used a flag-waving 'British' bulldog to promote its products in the jingoistic days just after the Boer War.

Hush Puppies®

Like the Labrador rescuing the little girl from drowning, Old Dog Tray tobacco was meant to be 'ever faithful' to its smokers. Alas, the smokers were less loyal.

In 1905, Spratt's dog biscuits (right) appealed elegantly to the owners of greyhounds, Saint Bernards and fluffy little terriers alike. Ten years earlier, Greensmith's dog biscuits (above) used a more exuberant, if rather more downmarket, approach to the sale of dog biscuits.

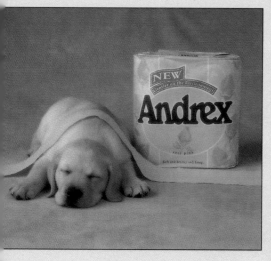

Perhaps the Labrador puppy was meant to be as 'soft and strong' as Andrex lavatory paper. Or perhaps the puppy was there because — what else can you show in an advertisement for lavatory paper?

Introduced in 1900,

His Master's Voice quickly became one of the most familiar images
in the world, the subject of numerous spoofs and parodies.

terrier of indeterminate ancestry, who made his debut as the icon of The Gramophone
Company in 1900. When Mark Barraud, a scene-painter at the Prince's Theatre in
Bristol, died he left Nipper to his brother Francis, also a painter, who exhibited with
modest success at the Royal Academy in London. The genesis of what is now the
most famous dog painting in the world – and certainly one of the most famous of all
paintings – is fogged with anecdote and apocrypha. However, it is clear that Barraud
painted a portrait of Nipper, with ear cocked and bemused expression, listening to a
recording being played on an Edison cylinder phonograph. Aware of the commercial
possibilities of his picture, Barraud copyrighted it and asked the Edison Company if
they would like to buy it. This was sound nineteenth-century commercial practice.
The eminent Sir John Everett Millais had earned an enormous amount of money

One of the sledge dogs of
Robert Falcon Scott's Antarctic expedition listens to a frozen gramophone
in imitation of Francis Barraud's painting.

when his *Bubbles* (1886), a painting of a little boy, was used by the Pears soap company for their advertising campaign. Distressingly for Barraud, the Edison Company replied with a firm 'no'. He offered it to the Royal Academy for exhibition but, to his chagrin, the Academy found it somewhat lacking. He then altered the twice-rejected painting, replacing the Edison phonograph with a competing product, the flat disc gramophone. He offered this to The Gramophone Company who responded enthusiastically, paid Barraud £100 and adopted *His Master's Voice* as their corporate image. Barraud spent virtually the rest of his life painting copies of it.

Its obvious appeal made *His Master's Voice* an instant visual cliché. But, like all images that capture the imagination, there is more to it than a scrappy little dog unable to tell the difference between a recording and the real thing. The art historian

Robert Rosenblum unearthed The Gramophone Company's own explanation of the image's power: 'The strong appeal of the picture lies probably in the fidelity of the dog,' they wrote. 'It is appropriate, therefore, that this quality of fidelity has been the keynote of "His Master's Voice" ever since – fidelity in the reproduction of the works of great musical artists – fidelity to the public who have relied upon "His Master's Voice" for half a century to provide the latest and best in home entertainment.' I cannot help thinking that there is also an attempt to imbue consumers with dog-like fidelity to a brand.

Barraud neatly bridges the high art of painting with the 'low' arts of advertising and huckstership. Nipper's behaviour is not a million miles away from that of the mournful dogs attached to dead masters who inspired paintings like Breton Rivière's *Requiescat* (1889) in which a bloodhound grieves by the bier of a dead knight or, even more heartbreakingly, Sir Edwin Landseer's *The Old Shepherd's Chief Mourner* in which a dog nuzzles the coffin of his late owner long after the human mourners have gone.

The sternly intellectual Victorian critic John Ruskin was nearly in tears as he described 'the close pressure of the dog's breast against the wood, the convulsive clinging of the paws ... the fixed and tearful fall of the eye in its utter hopelessness, the rigidity of repose which marks that there had been no motion or change in the trance of agony since the last blow was struck on the coffin lid.' Ruskin continued to pile on the lugubrious detail describing 'how lonely has been the life, how unwatched the departure of him who is now laid solitary in his sleep ...'

The theme of the dog as mourner – particularly of those who used to be called 'the humble' – was a nineteenth-century favourite. It appealed both to their fascination with death and their desire to ascribe human attributes and emotions to animals. Before Hollywood made Rin-Tin-Tin famous, the most widely known dog in the world was probably Greyfriars Bobby, a Skye terrier who kept vigil at his late master's grave in Edinburgh from 1858 to 1872. Bobby was presented with a collar by the Lord Provost of Edinburgh and photographed and painted. After his death a memorial was put up to him by the philanthropic Lady Burdett-Coutts. He was also the subject of

Obsessed with mourning, the Victorians enjoyed the rich symbolism of a dog's loyalty to its dead master. Sir Edwin Landseer's schmaltzy *The Old Shepherd's Chief Mourner* (*left*) was a hugely popular icon of canine devotion; Greyfriar's Bobby (*right*) – the little Skye terrier who guarded his humble master's Edinburgh grave – was probably the first true canine celebrity.

a 1912 novel by Eleanor Atkinson which gave birth to a number of film versions including a weepie produced by Disney.

THE 'LEONARDO OF DOGS'

All the starring dogs of the mass media, from Rin-Tin-Tin to the Texaco fire dog and Snoopy the ubiquitous cartoon beagle, are the progeny of Sir Edwin Landseer, the Olympian creator of *The Old Shepherd's Chief Mourner*. Known as the 'Leonardo of dogs' he combined a dashing technique with the ability to turn the dogs he painted into individuals who directly engaged the emotions of the public. We have seen how he reduced John Ruskin – who memorably said of the far greater painter James McNeill Whistler that he 'never expected to hear a coxcomb ask two hundred guineas for flinging a pot of paint in the public's face' – to a quivering emotional wreck. Imagine Landseer's effect on less obdurate viewers.

He was born in 1802, into an artistic family. His father and one of his brothers were engravers, another brother was a painter and his two sisters painted miniatures. He exhibited at the Royal Academy as a teenager and began a lucrative career painting animals for the aristocracy. But the watershed for Landseer was an 1836 commission from the Duchess of Kent to paint her seventeen-year-old daughter's favourite dog Dash, a King Charles spaniel. The following year the duchess' daughter

The right artist in the right place at the right time: Landseer's extraordinary ability to paint animals with panache and just a hint of human emotion coincided with Queen Victoria's love of dogs. The result was a fortune and a knighthood for Landseer and a series of dog paintings that remain breathtaking. The coquettish Dash (*left*) was the young Victoria's favourite dog; Prince Albert's greyhound Eos (*right*) has a regal authority that any human monarch would be proud of.

came to the throne as Queen Victoria. Her long reign profoundly affected the popularity and status of dogs and made the young Landseer dog painter *par excellence* to the world. Engravings of his paintings sold tens of thousands of copies and made him familiar to a large middlebrow audience who could not even dream of affording one of his originals.

In his portrait of Dash a little dog has been invested with regal dignity as well as – to modern eyes – a liberal amount of sex appeal. It has been remarked that Landseer painted the dog in an intense, close-up manner, which brings to mind Orson Welles' remark that, 'There is indeed such a thing as a close-up actor. He's the one who doesn't score unless you frame him just under the chin. Rin-Tin-Tin and Lassie are good examples of the type.' Five years later Landseer painted a portrait of Prince Albert's favourite dog Eos, a black and white greyhound bitch. To me, at any rate, this is the Everest of formal dog portraiture – and not just because of its masterful

In *Laying Down the Law* (*above*),
Landseer used dogs to lampoon the Victorian legal system.
The dogs act out human roles with sure-footed hilarity – as they,
and other animals, do in Disney cartoons.

Landseer used dogs to comment on the
state of human society. *High Life and Low Life* (*previous page*), a pair of pictures
of a tough, no-nonsense working-class bulldog and a languidly aristocratic deerhound, is
a social portrait of a divided England – even if it is celebratory rather than critical.

composition and colouring. Here we see the dog as more than a mere animal, however pretty. Eos not only participates in the glamour and potency of his royal master, he has himself become a member of royalty. The picture decorated Prince Albert's dressing-room at Buckingham Palace.

Landseer may be seen by some as either a glamorizer or an apologist for the Establishment. Some of his paintings veer towards, and even arrive at, the sort of cuteness that makes unrestrained anthropomorphism hard to stomach. But he was unafraid to observe and comment on Victorian society through the allegorical use of dogs. In one pair of pictures *High Life and Low Life* – which may incidentally have inspired Disney's *The Lady and the Tramp* – he contrasts the proletarian bulldog with the aristocratic deerhound. Most remarkably, he savagely ridicules the legal system in *Laying Down the Law*, a courtroom drama enacted by a poodle, a mastiff, a spaniel, a bloodhound and a number of other breeds. This painting is the archetype for a thousand less brilliant images where dogs are seen to behave like humans. 'Landseer gives his beloved animals soul, thought, poetry and passion,' the French poet Théophile Gautier observed. 'He endows them with an intellectual life almost like our own ...'

ROYAL DOGS AND 'FIRST DOGS'

Landseer's numerous portraits of Queen Victoria's dogs – whether on their own or posing with their mistress – are part of a tradition that goes back 4000 years to the Antef stele we discussed in Chapter Three. Dogs of the great have been an intrinsic part of the iconography of power for a number of convincing reasons. Their simple affection can be a comfort from the Byzantine machinations of any court and monarchs in particular used the fidelity of their pets as object lessons for their sometimes unruly subjects. Dogs added warmth and normality to those who were sometimes aloof, and consequently became useful political tools.

Victoria was the most dog-loving head of state in modern times as well as perhaps the least acute at political image-making. Her disingenuous and unconditional devotion to her pets was remarkable even by the standards of the dog-loving British monarchs who went before her. For her Stuart predecessors, dogs were sometimes politically contentious. When James VI of Scotland ascended the English throne as James I he was vilified because he was foreign, possibly homosexual and suspect for the way in which he brought dogs firmly into the centre of court life. He was sometimes accused

of being more solicitous of them than of his subjects. His grandson Charles II would distractedly play with his many spaniels at the council table while matters of state were being discussed. 'God save your Majesty,' an exasperated courtier observed, 'but God damn your dogs.'

Victoria would have been at her most stonily unamused by any attack on her Pekingese, Pomeranians or Skye terriers. As she became more remote and withdrawn during her long widowhood, her care and concern for the royal dogs grew even more intense. Did Max Beerbohm have the old queen in mind when he wrote, 'You will find that the woman who is really kind to dogs is always one who has failed to inspire sympathy in men.'

In the United States the presidential pet – only half jocularly known as 'the first dog' – grew into as indispensable a part of the presidential public relations machine as kissing babies on the campaign trail. As a colonial country gentleman, George Washington maintained a household full of dogs. Captain, Cloe, Forester, Madame Moose and Sweetlips were just a few of them. Many successive American presidents were also dog owners, but in the United States the political manipulation of dogs is essentially a twentieth-century phenomenon.

Franklin Delano Roosevelt, the most genuinely patrician of all modern presidents, rarely went anywhere without his Scottish terrier Fala. His attachment to his Scottie was well known from the dog's frequent appearances in presidential photographs, and during the 1944 election campaign Roosevelt's Republican Party opponents began a scurrilous rumour. It was that the president had dispatched – at great cost and at the taxpayer's expense – a destroyer to the Aleutian Islands to fetch the dog, who had been somehow left behind after a presidential visit. Roosevelt counter-attacked ferociously and funnily in a national radio broadcast: 'These Republican leaders have not been content with attacks on me, my wife or on my sons. No, not content with that they now include my little dog, Fala. Well of course I don't resent such attacks

On 27 April 1964 the American president Lyndon Johnson shocked dog lovers when he vigorously tugged the ears of Him and Her, the White House beagles. While the animals yelped, he remarked that it 'does them good'. As with many dog owners, LBJ's choice of pet reflected his own looks.

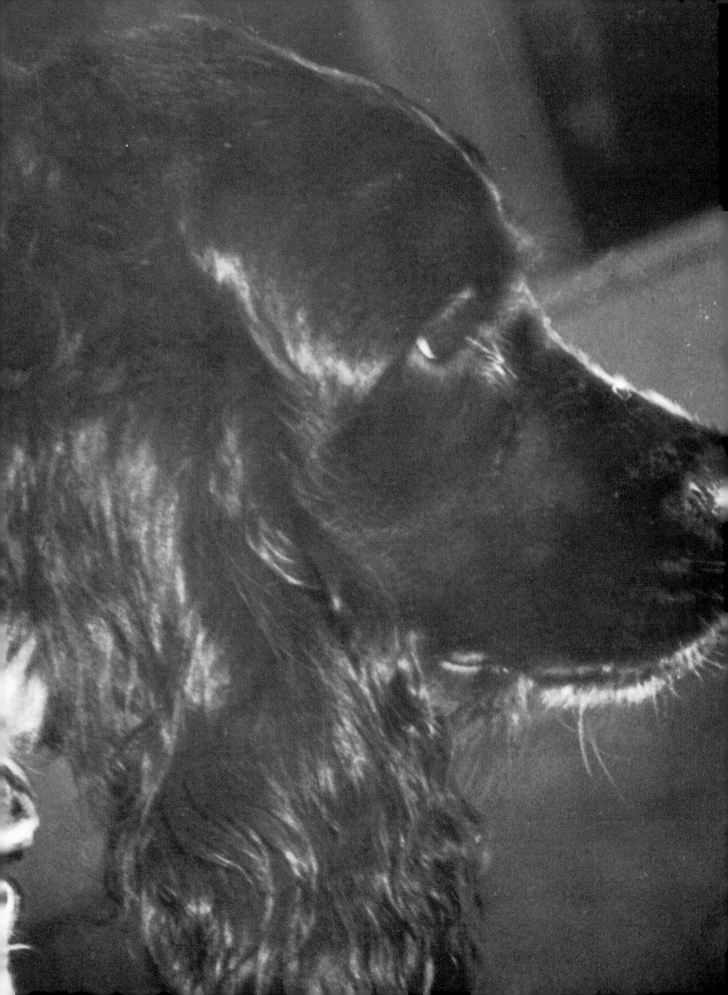

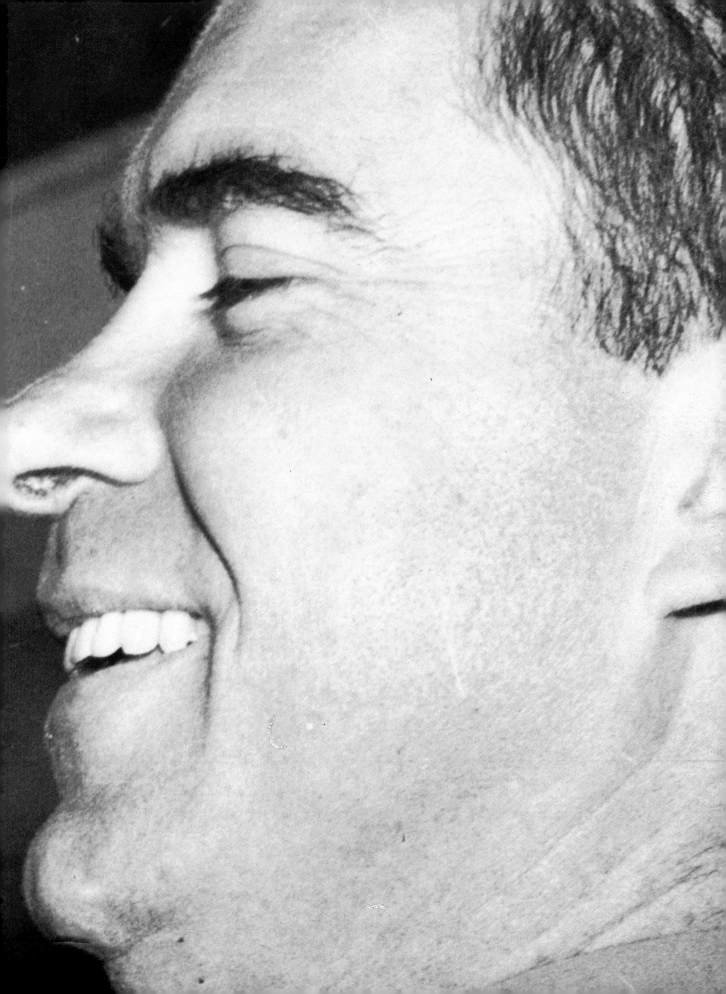

and my family doesn't resent attacks, but Fala does. You know Fala is Scotch and being a Scottie, as soon as he learned that the Republican fiction writers in Congress and out had concocted a story that I had left him behind on the Aleutian Islands and had sent a destroyer back to find him at a cost to the taxpayers of two or three or eight or twenty million dollars – his Scotch soul was furious. He has not been the same dog since.'

As a politician with a flair for getting into trouble and a ratlike cunning for getting out of it, Richard Nixon used the newly acquired family dog to extricate himself from what might have been a politically fatal scandal early in his career. As a young, Red-baiting Republican congressman from California, he was teamed up with elder statesman and war hero Dwight Eisenhower to form a political dream team in the 1952 presidential elections. But Eisenhower's smooth path to the White House was threatened by allegations that his vice-presidential running mate was accepting illegal campaign contributions. An indignant Nixon appeared on national television, vehemently denying all rumours of covert gifts and contributions. There was one gift from a well-wisher, he admitted. It was well known that the Nixon children wanted a puppy, so imagine the surprise and delight when a large crate was delivered to the Nixon house. 'Someone in Texas had sent us a little black and white cocker spaniel puppy,' Nixon admitted in a voice choked with mock emotion. 'My daughter had named it Checkers ... and I said that regardless of what anyone said about it, I was going to keep it.' Nixon brilliantly used a child and her puppy to deliver a devastating one-two punch to his opponents. The road that eventually led to Watergate and a nation's shame was paved with duplicity. Thankfully, it was not the dog's fault.

President Roosevelt (*left*)
saw off his opponents in a radio broadcast when they spread
the rumour that he had sent a destroyer to collect his
Scottie, Fala, from the Aleutian Islands.

Senator Richard Nixon rubs
noses with Checkers (*previous page*), the cocker spaniel who helped him out of a political
scandal in 1952. Accused of receiving illegal gifts, Nixon admitted he had accepted 'a little black
and white cocker spaniel puppy' and said that no one would take it away from his family.

EPILOGUE

One day in 1912, the German painter Franz Marc, his wife and dog went out for a walk in the Bavarian Alpine village of Sindelsdorf. They stopped at a picturesque spot, rested and admired the view. Marc noted the intense concentration with which his hound, Russi, stared at the landscape. He turned to his wife and said, 'I'd like to know for once what goes on inside that dog when he sits there and contemplates the landscape!' Back in his studio he painted *The Dog in Front of the World*, a painting which captures, maybe more brilliantly than any other work of art, the dog's role as a link between man and nature.

Another German, Arthur Schopenhauer, wrote that, 'The dog stands to the man in the same relation as a glass goblet to a metal one and this helps greatly to endear the dog so much to us, for it affords us great pleasure to see all those inclinations and emotions which we so often conceal displayed simply and openly in him.' Its behaviour, Schopenhauer went on to observe, 'is characterized by a certain stamp of innocence in contrast to the conduct of men which is withdrawn from the innocence of nature by the entrance of reason . . .' To Schopenhauer and others, the dog is a reminder of an innocent, Edenic, past.

Dogs and men have grown up together and perhaps only the dog has been unspoiled by that growing up. Despite all the jewelled collars, sometimes absurd

Franz Marc's

The Dog in Front of the World, painted in 1912, is a powerful
visual embodiment of one of mankind's most unanswerable questions:
what do dogs really think of the world and their masters?

pampering, outlandish hair styles and often preposterous breeding it has been subjected to, it has remained close to nature. That closeness is a constant and useful reminder to humans that civilization is not, perhaps, everything.

We may admire the usefulness of the horse, the beauty of the cat or the intelligence of the porpoise, but it is the dog we love: our oldest and best friend. Our closest relative, the great ape – who is, indeed, almost our physiological and intellectual equal – is sometimes dignified as being 'almost human'. Our very distant cousin, the dog, has been made an honorary human with no questions asked. No other animal has been brought into the heart of the human family.

During the thousands of years in which man and dog have been partners, everything except the intensity of our relationship has changed. Once a semi-nomadic hunter-gatherer, man has become – in the post-industrial world – a mostly town-dwelling creature who buys, rather than finds or catches, what he needs. But our old hunting companion is still with us. Some people may say that there is little point having dogs in today's world. That they can be dangerous, dirty, inconvenient and an intolerable 'luxury' unsuited for life on a crowded and rather sick planet like Earth. The municipal authorities in Beijing banned the private ownership of dogs for reasons very like these. In an almost immediate response, a dog zoo was opened where deprived human residents of the city can look at various breeds behind bars and, for a small fee, take the dogs for a therapeutic walk in an enclosed area. Having invented our best friend, we are unlikely to ban or disinvent him. There is the possibility, though, that we may change him.

Reason might dictate, for example, that people who live in city centres will demand compact, barkless animals. I believe the possibility is a faint one and that love's blindness makes us behave otherwise. I often see a woman walking two inconveniently huge borzois down my central London street. However, we may see an end to the obsessive breeding that means too many dogs are condemned to lives of inconvenience and medical problems merely to satisfy the arbitrary requirements of some breed standards. The English animal behaviouralist James Serpel has speculated that in the future we will breed dogs more for behaviour than for looks. Whatever happens, many of us will still want to share our lives with them: perhaps it all comes down to the fact that without dogs the world would seem a lonely place for man.

We use dogs to mirror our passions, fears and fancies. We gaze at them and see

The wrinkly coats of young sharpeis made these rare Chinese fighting dogs distinctive 'fashion accessories' for Hollywood film stars in the 1980s. But will such dogs have a future when such a trend passes?

ourselves. Amiable and agreeable beasts, they are happy to be our looking-glass. We also see something we do not understand when we look at a dog. Jack London wrote that, 'At times it was like gazing into a human soul, to look into his eyes; and what I saw there frightened me and started all sorts of ideas in my own mind of reincarnation and all the rest. I tell you I sensed something big in that brute's eyes; there was a message there, but I wasn't big enough myself to catch it ... I don't know what it

People buy puppies – like
these Sealyham terriers – and are 'stuck' with dogs. More to the
point, perhaps, dogs are stuck with us. Will we become more
considerate of our obligations towards these honorary humans
as the world becomes more crowded and difficult to live in?

was, but it gave me a feeling of kinship all the same. Oh, no, not sentimental kinship. It was, rather, a kinship of equality.'

This book began by saying that after millennia of intimacy we still don't know why dogs wag their tails. I suppose it is because we don't *need* to know. Or perhaps the reason can be found in these words which the American playwright Eugene O'Neill put into the mouth of his favourite dog: 'No matter how deep my sleep I shall hear you and not all the power of death can keep my spirit from wagging a grateful tail.'

BIBLIOGRAPHY

It would be impossible to write about dogs without two indispensable reference books: *The Reader's Digest Illustrated Book of Dogs* (Reader's Digest, 1989) and *Miller's Anatomy of the Dog* (W.B. Saunders, 1979). It would also be difficult to write without acknowledging the inspiration of Brian Vesey-Fitzgerald's sparkling scholarship. Only principal works consulted are acknowledged in this bibliography; there is not enough room to cite either newspaper articles or interviews.

AMUNDSEN, ROALD *The South Pole* John Murray, 1912.

BALLARD, PETER *A Dog Is for Life* National Canine Defence League, 1990.

BARNES, JONATHAN ed. *The Complete Works of Aristotle* Princeton University Press, 1984.

BERKHARDT, V.R. *Chinese Creeds and Customs* South China Morning Post, 1966.

BYRD, RICHARD *Little America* G.P. Putnams and Sons, 1931.

CARR, RAYMOND *English Foxhunting* Oxford University Press, 1976.

CARRUTHERS, PETER *The Animals Issue* Cambridge University Press, 1992.

CLARKE, PAUL and LINZEY, ANDREW eds *Political Theory and Animal Rights* Pluto Press, 1990.

CLUTTON-BROCK, JULIET *A Natural History of Domesticated Mammals* Cambridge University Press/British Museum (Natural History), 1989.

COOPER, JILLY *Animals in War* Imperial War Museum, 1983.

COPPINGER, LORNA AND RAYMOND 'Dogs in sheep's clothing guard flocks' *Smithsonian*, April 1982.

DENNIS-BRYAN, KIM and CLUTTON-BROCK, JULIET *Dogs of the last hundred years at the British Museum (Natural History)* British Museum, 1988.

DUBOS, RENE *Louis Pasteur: Free Lance of Science* Da Capo, 1960.

FANSHAWE, JOHN, FRAME, LORY and

GINSBERG, JOSHUA 'The wild dog – Africa's vanishing carnivore' *Oryx*, July 1991.

FARRINGTON, JANE, MACKINNON, GABRIELA and SYMONS, DAVID *Man's Best Friend* Birmingham Museum and Art Gallery, 1991.

FRANKFORT, H et al *The Intellectual Adventure of Ancient Man* University of Chicago Press, 1977.

GENTRY, CHRISTINE *When Dogs Run Wild* McFarland, 1983.

GODDEN, RUMER *The Butterfly Lions* Macmillan, 1977.

GRAY, ERNEST H. *Dogs of War* Robert Hale, 1989.

GREEN, JEFFREY 'Reducing Predation with Guarding Animals' in *Predator Management in North Coastal California* University of California Press, 1990.

GUBBER, N.J. *The Nunamuit Eskimos: Hunters of the Caribou* Yale University Press, 1965.

HANDS, BARBARA *All About the West Highland White Terrier* Pelham Books, 1987.

HINES, LINDA 'Pets in Prison: A New Partnership' *California Veterinarian*, 1983.

ITZKOWITZ, D.C. *A Peculiar Privilege* Harvester, 1977.

JANSSEN, ROSALIND AND JACK *Egyptian Household Animals* Shire Egyptology, 1989.

JESSE, G.R. *Researches Into the History of the British Dog* Robert Hardwicke, 1866.

LORENZ, KONRAD *Man Meets Dog* Houghton Mifflin, 1955.

LURKER, MANFRED *The Gods and Symbols of Ancient Egypt* Thames and Hudson, 1991.

MACDONALD, D.W. *Rabies and Wildlife* Oxford University Press, 1980.

MACGREGOR, FORBES *Greyfriars Bobby: The Real Story at Last* Gordon Wright, 1990.

MORRIS, DESMOND *Dogwatching* Cape, 1986.

OSGOOD, C. *The Chinese: A Study of a Hong Kong Community* University of Arizona Press, 1975.

PATERSON, DAVID and PALMER, MARY eds.

The Status of Animals C A B International, 1990.

PENNY, N.B. 'Dead Dogs and Englishmen' *The Connoisseur*, August 1976.

PFERD III, WILLIAM *Dogs of the American Indians* Denlinger's, 1987.

READE, JULIAN *Assyrian Sculpture* British Museum, 1990.

RICHARDSON, E.H. *Forty Years with Dogs* Hutchinson, 1929.

RITVO, HARRIET *The Animal Estate* Penguin, 1990.

ROLLIN, BERNARD *The Unheeded Cry* Oxford University Press, 1989.

ROSENBLUM, ROBERT *The Dog in Art from Rococo to Post-Modernism* John Murray, 1988.

RUPKE, NICHOLAS ed. *Vivisection in Historical Perspective* Routledge, 1990.

SAVISHINSKY, JOEL S. 'The Child is Father to the Dog: Canines and Personality Processes in an Artic Community' *Human Development* 17: 1974.

SECORD, WILLIAM *Dog Painting 1840–1940* Antique Collectors' Club, 1992.

SMITH, JANE and BOYD, KENNETH eds. *Lives in the Balance* Oxford University Press, 1991.

STAGER, LAWRENCE *Ashkelon Discovered* Biblical Archaeological Society, 1991.

STOVER, ERIC and CHARLES, DAN 'The killing minefields of Cambodia' *New Scientist*, 19 October 1991.

THOMAS, KEITH *Man and the Natural World* Penguin, 1984.

TREEN, ALFRED AND ESMERALDA *The New Dalmatian* Howell Book House, 1992.

TURNER, TREVOR ed. *Veterinary Notes for Dog Owners* Popular Dogs, 1990.

VARNER, JOHN AND JEANNETTE *Dogs of the Conquest* University of Oklahoma Press, 1983.

WATSON, J.N.P. *The Book of Foxhunting*, Batsford, 1977.

WILSON, EDWARD *Diary of the Terra Nova Expedition*, Blandford Press, 1972.

WINOKUR, JON *Mondo Canine* Dutton, 1991.

INDEX

PICTURE CREDITS

Page 2 Zefa; 7 Barnaby's Picture Library; 9 Bruce Coleman/Jane Burton; 12 Hulton Deutsch Collection; 13 Forbes Magazine Collection, New York/Bridgeman Art Library (detail from *On Guard, A Newfoundland Dog*, Richard Ansdell 1815–85); 15 British Museum/Werner Forman Archive; 16 Tate Gallery, London/Bridgeman Art Library; 18 Hulton Deutsch Collection; 20 *bottom left* Christie's Images, *bottom right* Bonhams; 20–1 *centre* Zefa/Lacz-Lemoin; 21 *top right* Michael Holford, *bottom right* Hulton Deutsch Collection; 22 British Musuem, London; 24 Mary Evans Picture Library; 25 Mansell Collection; 27 Staatliche Scholsser und Garten, Potsdam/Bridgeman Art Library; 28 The Board of Trustees of the National Museums & Galleries on Merseyside (Liverpool Museum); 31 Barnaby's Picture; 33 Mary Evans Picture Library; 34 Bruce Coleman/Stephen J. Krasemann; 35 *top* Zefa/Frans Lanting, *bottom* Zefa/David Corke; 38–9 Zefa/Jim Brandenburg; 41 Bruce Coleman/Rod Williams; 42 *left* Christie's Images, *top right* Mary Evans Picture Library, *centre right* Leeds Castle Museum; 42–3 *bottom* Leeds Castle Museum; 43 *top left* Galleria Palatina, Florence/Bridgeman Art Library (*Portrait of a Dog*, Giovanna Garzoni, 1600–70), *centre left* & *top right* Leeds Castle Museum, *bottom right* Mary Evans Picture Library; 47 F.R. Valla; 48–9 Bruce Coleman/Stephen J. Krasemann; 50 Barnaby's Picture Library; 53 Egyptian Musuem, Cairo/Henry G. Fischer; 54–5 Egyptian Museum, Cairo/Giraudon; 56 Ancient Art & Architecture Collection; 58 *left* Michael Holford, *top right* Louvre, Paris/Lauros-Giraudon/Bridgeman Art Library; 58–9 *bottom* British Library/Bridgeman Art Library; 59 *top left* Lauros-Giraudon/Bridgeman Art Library, *centre bottom* Louvre, Paris/Bridgeman Art Library, *right* Animal Photography/Sally Anne Thompson; 60 British Museum, London; 61 Egyptian Museum, Cairo/Robert Harding Picture Library; 64 Archiv für Kunst und Geschichte, Berlin; 66 Mansell Collection; 68 Museum of Saint-Germain-en-Laye/Archives R. Laffont/Franceschi; 69 Archaeological Museum, Naples/Giraudon; 71 British Museum, London; 72–3 *top* Verulamium Museum, St. Albans; 73 *bottom* Private collection. Reproduced by permission of Thames & Hudson Ltd; 75 Christie's, London/Bridgeman Art Library; 78 Bruce Coleman/Fritz Prenzel; 79 British Museum, London; 81 National Gallery, London; 83 Mary Evans Picture Library/Sigmund Freud Copyrights; 84 *top* Stephanie Hoppen Ltd, *bottom left* National Museum of American Art/Smithsonian Institution/Bridgeman Art Library, *bottom right* British Museum/Michael Holford; 85 *top* Bibliothèque Nationale, Paris, *bottom left* Stephanie Hoppen Ltd, *bottom right* Benaki Museum, Athens/Scala; 86 Society S. Giorgio degli Sciavone, Venice/E. T. Archive; 87 Sistine Chapel, Vatican/Scala; 88 British Museum, London; 89 Hulton Deutsch Collection; 90 Union Pictures/Pratap Rughani; 92 from *Mowgli's Brothers* by Rudyard Kipling, illustrated by Christopher Wormell, pub. HarperCollins Publishers Ltd 1992; 93 Leeds City Museum; 94 Zefa; 95 Australian Overseas Information Service, London; 96 By Courtesy of the Dean & Chapter of Westminster; 97 Liverpool Museum/Werner Forman Archive; 99 B & C. Alexander; 100–1 Zefa/J. Bitsch; 104 & 105 Scott Polar Research Institute; 108 Mary Evans Picture Library; 109 Zefa/Villiger; 110 Peter Newark's Western Americana; 111 Mary Evans Picture Library; 112 Westminster Abbey Library; 113 David Woodfall; 114 Animals Animals; 116 *top left* & *bottom right* Union Pictures/Pratap Rughani, *centre* Animal Photography/ Sally Anne Thompson; 117 *all* Union Pictures/Pratap Rughani; 118–9 Barbara Hands; 120 Mary Evans Picture Library; 121 Zefa/W. L. Hamilton; 123 Scala; 124 Imperial War Museum; 128 *left* Framed Philatelics; 128–9 *centre* Spectrum Colour Library; 129 *right* Framed Philatelics; 130 Hulton Deutsch Collection; 133 Animal Photography/Sally Anne Thompson; 134 *left* Museo de Arte, Sao Paolo/ Bridgeman Art Library (detail from *The Temptation of St Anthony*, Hieronymus Bosch, c. 1450–1516), *right* Animal Photography/Sally Anne Thompson; 135 *left* St George's Chapel, Windsor, *right* Animal Photography/Sally Anne Thompson; 137 Bettmann Archive; 138 Animal Photography/R. Willbie; 141 Musée Condé, Chantilly/Bridgeman Art Library; 142 Bargello, Florence/Scala; 144–5 Musée des Augustine, Toulouse/Giraudon; 146 Château Fontainebleu/Giraudon; 148 *top* Christie's Images, *bottom left* Phillips Fine Art Auctioneers; 148–9 *centre* & 149 *top right* Christie's Images; 149 *bottom right* Phillips Fine Art Auctioneers; 150 Bury Art Gallery/Bridgeman Art Library (*Gamekeeper with Dogs*, Richard Ansdell, 1815–85); 151 B. & C. Alexander; 153 Gavin Graham Gallery/Bridgeman Art Library (*On the Scent*, Heywood Hardy, 1843–1933); 154–5 Bruce Coleman/Rex Coleman; 158 Oldham Art Gallery/Bridgeman Art Library; 160 Hutchinson Library; 161 Allsport; 163 Wellcome Institute Library, London; 165 Ref. 53.91r: opaque colour & gold on paper. Courtesy of the Freer Gallery of Art, Smithsonian Institution, Washington D.C.; 166–7 Musée Condé, Chantilly/Bridgeman Art Library; 169 Musée d'Orsay, Paris/Giraudon; 173 *top* Granger Collection, *bottom left* The Royal Collection © 1993 Her Majesty the Queen, *bottom right* Popperfoto; 174 Zefa; 176 *top* oil on canvas $35\frac{3}{8}'' \times 43\frac{1}{4}''$. Albright-Knox Art Gallery, Buffalo, New York. Bequest of A. Conger Goodyear & Gift of George F. Goodyear 1964 *bottom left* Musée de la Chartreuse/Giraudon/Bridgeman Art Library (detail from *Two Dogs in a Park*, Abraham van den Tempel, (1620–72) *bottom right* Iona Antiques, London; 177 *top left* Victoria & Albert Museum/Michael Holford, *centre left* National Gallery, London, *bottom left* Iona Antiques, London, *right* Bruce Coleman/Hans Reinhard; 179 Animal Photography/Sally Anne Thompson; 181 Hulton Deutsch Collection; 182 Kobal Collection; 184 © Disney; 185 Animals Animals; 187 ICI; 188 *left* Mary Evans Picture Library, *right* British Shoe; 189 *both top* Mary Evans Picture Library, *bottom left* Scott Ltd, *bottom right* Archiv für Kunst und Geschichte, Berlin; 190 EMI; 191 Popperfoto; 192 Victoria & Albert Museum/Bridgeman Art Library; 193 Popperfoto; 194, 195 The Royal Collection © 1993 Her Majesty the Queen; 196, 197 Tate Gallery, London; 198 Devonshire Collection, Chatsworth. Reproduced by permission of the Chatsworth Settlement Trustees; 200 UPI/Bettmann; 202 Popperfoto; 204–5 UPI/Bettmann; 207 Private coll., Switzerland; 209 Zefa/ Wegler; 210–1 Animal Photography/Sally Anne Thompson.